rick

tudio
2.2016–06.2016
msterdam, Vaduz

rawings 1:10
2–15.03.2016
msterdam

Vorkshop
6–20.03.2016
zewijn

→ 34, 92, 132

→ 50, 102, 138

CRAFTING THE FAÇADE

STONE BRICK WOOD

Urs Meister,
Carmen Rist-Stadelmann,
Machiel Spaan (eds.)

PARK BOOKS

1 CRAFTING THE DRAWING

2 TECTONIC REFLECTION

3 NINE FAÇADES

4 CRAFTING STONE, BRICK AND WOOD HANDS-ON

Foreword

It is known that the unified work as a whole is greater than the sum of its parts. The added value of the whole becomes particularly visible in the strategic partnerships in the European Erasmus+ programme. The Institute of Architecture and Planning at the University of Liechtenstein, together with its cooperation partners—the Amsterdam Academy of Architecture and the Mackintosh School of Architecture in Glasgow—created significant added educational value that captivates students, lecturers and experts alike.

For three years, the three universities addressed the research question of what influence the materials brick, stone and wood have on the construction, design and appearance of façades. In the process, the connecting elements in the European context were compared and discussed.

To achieve this in the Netherlands, the United Kingdom and Liechtenstein, design studios were set up at all three partner universities and the same design tasks were performed in each. The focus was put on mutual learning about the different approaches to and perspectives on the topic. The outcomes that emerged in the form of design projects and oversized, hand-drawn façade drawings are surpassed by the European added value that all the project participants have come to know and value.

Liechtenstein's National Agency for Erasmus+ Higher Education recognizes the outstanding project management and excellent development performance of all three universities with regard not only to architecture and spatial development, but also to how the work promotes European values.

The project 'Crafting the Façade' is a festive climax to an exciting European educational journey that focuses on the highest forms of knowledge transfer between international students and lecturers.

Stefan Sohler,
Director of the National Agency

Clarissa Frommelt,
Head of Erasmus+ Higher Education

Introduction

Carmen Rist-Stadelman,
Urs Meister

This publication represents a summary of our three-year Erasmus+ partnership involving three universities—the Amsterdam Academy of Architecture, the Mackintosh School of Architecture in Glasgow and the University of Liechtenstein—which was funded by the EU to examine building envelopes against the backdrop of varied architectural traditions. The aim of the project partnership was to generally promote a structural and material examination of our European buildings, not only focusing on architectural and constructional issues, but also allowing cultural, social and economic aspects to flow into the work.

Today, an increasing number of factors determine the configuration of an aesthetically and functionally high-quality building envelope, above all the requirement for first-class quality in terms of energy use. As such, it has become difficult today to obtain architectural form from the logic of one single building material. The architectural task is rapidly breaking up into highly diverse, particular technical subjects that are clearly manifest in the complex configuration of façades. While the individual layers resolve their respective task discretely and brilliantly, their interplay with one another often reveals the fundamental shortcomings of material expression. By letting go of what were formerly inseparably unified categories in architecture, we are faced today with the threat of losing the culture of building and the difficulty of establishing a coherent architectural language from construction becomes apparent.

By choosing the materials stone, brick and wood, we placed a clear focus on the building traditions present in the three countries. We analysed existing buildings, constructive elements and façade materials, examined artisanal traditions and technical aspects, and learned from our vernacular buildings in order to draw lessons for the future. Against the backdrop of climate change and the imperative to build in a way that saves resources, these topics enable us to redefine how existing and new building envelopes shall be treated, thus fulfilling the European Commission's long-term goals for creating intelligent, sustainable and resource-efficient projects and, in the process, enriching the European discourse.

The design studios were at the heart of the project partnership, complemented by joint workshops and joined together to make up a new whole. Each of the three project partners was responsible for the content and organization of one design task, which was then carried out jointly. In this way, an important architectural, cultural and social exchange took place within the European educational landscape. In times of internationalization, this represents a valuable contribution towards raising awareness of our building culture and is of great importance, both in teaching and in the building industry, as well as in the area of politics. The symposium held during the term of the project also made our experiences and outcomes available to interested parties outside of the project partnerships.

This publication makes no claim to be complete, and it should instead be understood as a contribution to the discussion concerning façades. It serves to enrich the current European discussion about building envelopes and their importance within the context of technology, building culture and the social realm.

1 CRAFTING THE DRAWING

The Architectural Drawing as a Didactic Tool

Carmen Rist-Stadelmann

The demands placed on an architectural drawing are complex. For instance, it offers architects the ability to examine the impact of their designs; it provides clients with a visual impression; it enables competition jurors to make comparisons and selections; and it provides contractors with information for turning the idea into reality.[1] How have the ways of depicting the architectural drawing changed over time and what importance did it have in architectural education? This line of questioning developed during the course of the 'Crafting the Façade' project.

The architectural drawing as a unique art of representation

At the beginning of the 18th century, an independent, gradual evolution and autonomization of the architectural drawing can be perceived, and it emerges as competition to classical painting. The fantastic architectural illustrations of Giovanni Battista Piranesi, with his beguiling depictions of an idealized architecture, have undoubtedly contributed to this. The grisaille technique he used, a monochrome painting technique using only shades of grey that depicts shadows to give the volumes a vivid and architectural appearance, underscores the magical impact of these architectural drawings.[2]

The revolutionary architectural designs of Étienne-Louis Boullée too, also made with the grisaille technique, became known all across Europe through publication in various sources, and they had far-reaching influence on the further depiction and quality of architectural drawings. The high quality of architectural drawing as practised in France and Italy, however, did not predominate in all European countries. This was achieved in Germany by paying particular attention in architectural education to the training of drawing skills. In newly established and reformed academies and building schools in Berlin and Munich, for example, geometrical drawing with light and shadow was taught in the first stage of education. Perspective was then taught in the second stage, and in the third stage, proportions, symmetry and the classical order were taught, entirely in line with the 18th-century understanding of the architecture of the ancient world as the basis of all architectural knowledge.[3]

At the beginning of the 19th century, presentation techniques in architectural drawing changed in Germany by turning away from the Vitruvian doctrine and moving towards a new level of reality and illusion, as promoted by Karl Friedrich Schinkel and Leo von Klenze. According to their notions, architecture should not just be built to protect against cold and moisture, but also merge with its surroundings into a new whole. This poetic exaggeration of architecture led to coloured drawings that integrated a perfect depiction of architecture and its surroundings in a realistic architectural drawing. The establishment of this type of depiction was further reinforced by the introduction of public competitions in Germany and Austria, leading to an increase in the picturesque quality of architectural drawings. This type of architectural drawing was easy for laypeople to read and also illustrated the ideas

1 Gerd Albers, foreword in: Winfried Nerdinger, *Die Architekturzeichnung*, Munich (Prestel) 1986, 2nd ed., p. 6.
2 Werner Oechslin, 'From Piranesi to Libeskind—Explaining by Drawing', in: *Daidalos*, 1981, No. 1, pp. 15–19.
3 Winfried Nerdinger, *Die Architekturzeichnung*, Munich (Prestel) 1986, 2nd ed., p. 8.

realistically, with the existing surroundings. Architecture was no longer presented in isolation in the drawing, becoming instead part of the reality.[4]

In the second half of the 19th century, Friedrich von Thiersch supplemented the picturesque manner of representation with constructive elements. In his drawings, he combined a plan, section and perspective and watercoloured these drawings in order to give them a structurally realistic yet picturesque appearance. With this presentation means, he combined drawing and watercolour techniques so masterfully that he won numerous competitions.[5] This type of depiction of the façade, the combination and interplay of section and elevation in one architectural drawing, was also used in the 'Crafting the Façade' programme. The scale of 1:10 for the façade drawings, which was settled upon over the course of the process, turned out to be optimal because it enabled, indeed required, the students to deal directly with the material to resolve the constructional and artistic aspects of the designed façade and to depict its tectonic attributes.

The increasing criticism of the historicism dominant in the 18th and 19th centuries is also reflected in architectural drawings at the beginning of the 20th century. Thus the freehand drawing, made without a straight edge and executed in India ink, corresponded more to the new idea of an emerging Art Nouveau style than the vibrant watercolours of the 19th century. In keeping with the expressionist architecture of the 1920s and 1930s, the use of drawing charcoal, with its distinctive and characteristic line, found increased use in architectural drawings. The picturesque architectural drawing of the previous two centuries had become obsolete.

The architectural drawing in competition with photography and computers

The rise of photography, which, beginning in the mid-19th century increasingly became competition to painting, accelerated the departure from the realistic, romantic architectural drawing to an unemotional representation. Despite their rational appearance, the architectural drawings of the early 20th century possessed a highly graphic quality, as they were still predominantly made with the drawing traditions of the 19th century. This can also be ascribed to the continued connection to and use in teaching the architectural curriculum. With the advent of modernism, however, this tradition of drawing was disregarded more and more, indeed almost disparaged. The axonometric view and floor plan were given primacy over façade and perspective. At the same time, the focus shifted from the façades to the plans and their depiction. This departure is not surprising, coming as it did after the many discussions about the right style and about the issues surrounding the façade architecture of the 19th century. Le Corbusier observed:

> *The plan is the determining factor for the whole. It is the decisive moment. A plan is not a pretty thing to draw, like a Madonna's face. It is a severe abstraction, nothing but dry mathematics for the eye. But the work of the mathematician remains one of the highest activities of the human mind.*[6]

At the same time, courses and exercises that trained freehand drawing and nurtured the culture of architectural drawing increasingly disappeared from architectural education.

With the advent of computers, architectural drawing was increasingly deprived of its true foundation and meaning. What was once a unique art of representation has now been overtaken by countless renderings and image processing applications. The resulting loss of architectural drawing can no longer be overlooked at the beginning of the 21st century and increasingly led to a kind of countermovement in which work that is graphic, handcrafted and artisanal is again in demand and is now being bolstered. Yet it makes no sense to call into question the importance of computers for architecture today or to fight against it out of romanticizing beliefs. We must simply be cognizant of its limitations and pay increased attention to its sensible application.

The computer is a contemporary tool that needs to be used sensibly. It can never supplant the sensuous and haptic experiences in the interplay of hand and brain when making a drawing, nor can it offer the knowledge gained in working with materials at full scale.

A drawing is the outcome of the interplay between observation and expression, between hand and head. It reveals the individual and characteristic expression of an idea and reflects its maker's concept. And this individual expression is precisely what is lost with renderings and image processing applications. The architectural drawing of today looks the same all over the world, because everyone more or less works with and uses the same computer programs. That is why it was all the more surprising to see the perseverance and enjoyment with which the students sketched, drew and coloured their façade elevations and sections by hand as part of the 'Crafting the Façade' programme. Without doubt, the effort involved was many times greater than generating it by computer, but the visible satisfaction and the glowing pride in the students spoke for themselves. From a didactic point of view, this is an important aspect within architectural education, since the students also explained that they needed to do more thinking when drawing by hand, because each line of the drawing gives that drawing its character and because the drawing is ultimately the sum of each individual action. Of course every line generated by the computer has its importance, but the interplay of the hand and the brain is more appreciable with freehand drawings and the result is not immediately interchangeable in the individual drawing.

Learning through experience

Pallasmaa aptly describes this in *The Thinking Hand* as follows:

> *In drawing by hand and pencil/pen, the hand follows the outlines, shapes and patterns of the object, whereas when drawing by mouse and computer, the hand usually selects the lines from a given set of symbols that have no analogical—or, consequently, haptic or emotional—relation to the object of drawing. Whereas the hand drawing is a mimetic moulding of lines, shades and tones, the computer drawing is a mediated construction.*[7]

In his teaching at the Bauhaus, Josef Albers had already anchored learning in experience, remarking:

> *Looking over the results of these experiments, we often realize afterwards that seeming innovations already exist. But the result is the student's own experience and possession, because it has been learned rather than taught. Learning is better than teaching because it is more intensive: the more we teach, the less students can learn.*[8]

Learning through experience, whether it is achieved by drawing elevations and sections of existing and newly developed façades built with the materials stone, brick and wood, as in our case, or by experimenting with the materials wood and brick at a scale of 1:1, provided the characteristic and likewise important didactic moment of our three-year programme. The façade and the architectural drawing serve as a framework for learning through experience, whose insights are visible in the students' large, metre-long drawings. For centuries, architectural drawing has played a significant role in the architectural profession and, not surprisingly, was therefore also strongly anchored in architectural education. Changes in the zeitgeist, innovations in construction, technical developments and the architect's own personal idiosyncrasies nearly led this art of representation to fall into oblivion. The time now seems ripe to remind ourselves of its importance, to discuss the broad spectrum of its depiction, and to once again increasingly cultivate the architectural drawing as a tool for architectural education.

4 Winfried Nerdinger, *Die Architekturzeichnung*, Munich (Prestel) 1986, 2nd ed., pp. 8–10.
5 Winfried Nerdinger, *Die Architekturzeichnung*, Munich (Prestel) 1986, 2nd ed., pp. 13–14.
6 Adolf Behne, *Der moderne Zweckbau*, Berlin (Ullstein) 1964; trans. by Michael F. Robinson as: *The Modern Functional Building*, Los Angeles (Getty Research Institute) 1996, p. 132.
7 Juhani Pallasmaa, *The Thinking Hand: Existential and Embodied Wisdom in Architecture*, Chichester (John Wiley & Sons) 2009, p. 97.
8 Josef Albers, 'Werklicher Formunterricht', *Bauhaus 2/3* (1928), transl. by Frederick Amrine, Frederick Horowitz, and Nathan Horowitz, available online: http://www.albersfoundation.org/teaching/josef-albers/texts/

Drawings as Instruments of Knowledge

Alan Hooper

The context for the first of the 'Crafting the Façade' workshops, held from 10 to 17 October 2015, was Glasgow's 19th-century gridded urban core. Our material was stone and the task was, to say the least, challenging. What meaningful knowledge could students gain about such a difficult and demanding material as stone in a week-long workshop? Stone goes back a long way, a testament to its geological production over deep time, measured in millennia rather than weeks. The material properties of stone—hard, heavy, brittle—demand commitment and time from those who seek to master the material. The craft knowledge of the stonemason, like his material, developed over millennia and passed from generation to generation. In recognition of the inherent difficulties of developing understanding by working directly with stone within the restricted timeframe of the workshop, the focus shifted to the observation of stone through the act of drawing. The intention was to explore stone culture as manifest in Glasgow's urban buildings, through drawing selected stone façades from various periods that show a range of stone construction techniques. However, even at the outset of the workshop fundamental questions remained. What kind of drawings would be appropriate? And, given that the workshop was to be a collaborative endeavour, how might students produce a drawing or drawings in a collaborative manner?

On the opening days of the workshop, field trips, building visits and lectures were offered as stimuli to engage students both in the material properties of stone and in the expression of a built stone culture within Glasgow. But the pedagogical intent and learning value of workshop remained unclear. Then, around the second or third day of the workshop, a serendipitous discovery: SCALE. What if students drew the selected buildings at an unusually large scale, with all the attendant difficulties of making very large drawings? Initial thoughts were to draw continuous sections through the façades at scale 1:20, then the decision to shift the scale to 1:10, necessitating the 'construction' of drawings up to five metres in length—drawings that would not only raise significant questions about how the façades of the selected buildings were constructed, but of equal pedagogical importance, how to make drawings of such a size. For students whose architectural education is predicated on the physical limitations and virtual freedom of the computer screen, making physical drawings of this size was new territory, requiring the development of new drawing skills and techniques. Charles and Ray Eames' seminal film *Powers of Ten* came to mind, an architectural meditation on scale and attendant questions that arise through microscopic and telescopic perspectives. The film begins with an image of the earth from outer space, an image that contains, but from a galactic perspective does not reveal, a man reclining on a picnic blanket in the middle of New York's Central Park. The film proceeds in magnifications of ten until the final images explore the biological structure of the human body at a molecular scale. Each stage of the journey from outer space to the anatomical construction of the human body reveal a series of worlds within worlds, each redolent with information waiting to be transformed into knowledge through investigation and understanding. Whilst exploring these individual micro-systems, the film is ultimately a meditation on connectedness and the wholeness of things. The film's message—that we need to perceive and comprehend at multiple scales at the same time—is fundamental to the conceptualization and production of meaningful architecture. As architect Glenn Howels presciently confirms, 'Architects must develop a design approach that allows many issues to be considered at different scales, simultaneously'. If the workshop timescale prohibited students from developing the necessary skills to work directly with stone, then they could at least grapple with the inherent difficulties of representing stone construction at a scale and size beyond their previous experience. The realization was that the production of big drawings would offer students valuable insights into the material qualities of stone and the construction of Glasgow's 'cliff-like' buildings, while overcoming the difficulties of making such drawings, which in turn echo the difficulties inherent with working with stone. Such difficulties can only be overcome by dedication and commitment to the task at hand and made possible through the acquisition of knowledge, development of skills and application of techniques. In essence, a form of craftsmanship akin to that of the stonemason. With the shift of drawing scale, the core value of the workshop was clarified. Students were offered fundamental insights into both the craft of making, be it a stone building or hand drawing, and of equal significance insight into the role of drawings as instruments of knowledge that fuse the conception and construction of buildings. Besides clarifying the value of the workshop, the increase in drawing scale marked a dramatic increase in production, as drawings of a scale alien to a generation of students restricted by the limits of computer screens began to appear. The size of the drawings required students to develop new skills and new techniques, new drawing materials in the form of charcoal, new drafting tools in the construction of large flat smooth drawing surfaces and the use of timber battens to draft construction lines for the final drawing. Given the students lack of experience in producing hand-made drawings of such a scale and size, the quality of initial drawings was relatively poor, and while the final drawings were less than masterly, the exponential rise in quality from the first to the last drawing iterations was extremely impressive. The student satisfaction in encountering and resolving difficulties of drawing production was palpable. Students discovered the value of the hand drawing as a crafted object unmediated by the computer, and staff were reminded that learning is a journey of adventure, where the end point is unknown at the outset and the output is less important than the process. While the contents of this publication reflect the drawings and sketches produced during the stone workshop in Glasgow, the true value of the workshop resides within the learning journey experienced by the participating staff and students—new knowledge that will undoubtedly inform the future practice of both staff and students.

Material, Scale and Drawing

Urs Meister

If the human being is the measure of all things when it comes to our sensory perception of the world, and if neither the notion of space nor that of architecture would exist without humans, then scale is what puts us in relation to the world of things. Scale gives us a visual reference with relation to space. Scale enables architecture to be immediately deciphered, thus giving us orientation in space. While the units of measurement, at least in Europe up to the period after the French Revolution, were lingually connected to human physiognomy through terms like ell, foot and span, the introduction of the metre did away with this relationship. Nevertheless, the inseparable link between our human bodies and the buildings and spaces around us lives on in the architectural scale.

Control over space

The Dutch monk and architect Dom Hans van der Laan developed his own theory about the scale of things, which he implemented in the monasteries he built. About this, Caroline Voet writes:

> *We 'read' our environment by relating objects to each other, by comparing and differentiating. If we understand by seeing, then we do this by measuring and gauging. We intuitively estimate the size of something by choosing a yardstick in the space and using it as a foundation for 'counting' this space.*[1]

The 'yardstick' is the measure of all things that we recognize, and between which we make connections. Whether in the tartan pattern of a fabric or the layout of a town, Van der Laan discovered and deciphered equal measures of rhythm and density in both. Fibre, thread and fabric are three stages in a production process that he likewise saw in architecture. "The fibre disappears into the thread, and the thread, in turn, into the cloth."[2] Variations in proportion and colour ultimately make it possible to reach a visual balance in the composition of the fabric, and this also applies when translated to achieving balance in a façade. It is not without reason that Van der Laan built his monasteries using brickwork, albeit with a whitewashed finish, in order to place the main focus on the ratio of masonry to opening. His absolute devotion to dimension, proportion and form ultimately led to his almost religious 'trinity' of space, form and measure. Using scale, he forged a connection between physical experience, sensory perception and intellectual knowledge of the gauging of space, and by so doing he ultimately formulated the human desire to gain control over space.

What a façade can tell us

A well-assembled façade allows us to intellectually penetrate the pores of the material, giving us points of reference from where we can continue to imagine the relationships between the parts. To do this, we must be able to see them from varying distances. From the perspective of the whole, where the façade must assert itself as part of the city with a characteristic expression that sets the building apart from its neighbours, and yet still allows it to enter into a dialogue while remaining distinct. From close up, where the parts of the building take advantage of their material qualities and reveal an internal order via the nature of how they are joined. And, finally, from inside, where openings share and regulate the connection to the urban or landscaped space outside. But we need an intermediary between our body and the building. The architectural detail can serve to translate the thing into a perception and offer points of reference for our eyes, which would otherwise helplessly scour the surfaces without deriving depth. The clever detail makes demands on us, reveals the characteristic and, in the best case, bears within its nucleus the essence of the whole. Thus paying attention to an articulated interface between two building parts, a well-produced transition from wall to opening, or a relief-like accent in the surface, makes profound sense in human terms. Seen from this perspective, 'Crafting the Façade' sheds light on the topic from two angles: from the production of the façade and its design on the one hand, and on the other, from the perspective of the observer, who has a right—with the help of the façade—to be able to read and understand the building. 'Crafting the Façade' aimed to grasp the façade as texture, on the level of which architecture is used as a means with which to weave a complex story from the relationship between components that are linked to one another.

The scale of the material

In its scale, *brick* is per se subject to the measure of the human hand, and also to the physical possibilities of the bricklayer (weight) and the conditions of production (firing process in the kiln). It is hard to imagine another material that has remained so consistent in its size as brick, and today's modern product is still very similar to the adobe or mud brick that is still made by hand throughout the world. The scale of *timber construction* comes from the dimensions of the tree trunk, which in pre-industrial times was processed by hand. In old log cabins, the heights of the horizontal timbers often vary depending on what could be cut down in the nearby woods. Although the timbers were also sequentially numbered so that entire buildings could be relocated, the wood used for building was, to the greatest extent possible, cut down, stored, processed and used locally. The scale of the tree trunk is, however, only recognizable and present in massive timber. Industrially processed wood such as glued laminated timber and plywood boards, due to the transverse veneering of the trunk and the lengthwise finger-jointing, and ultimately due to modern adhesive bonding techniques, is standardized in all its dimensions and structurally calculable, but has, as it were, come to also be without scale—we could also refer to it as domesticated timber. A *stone* building, by comparison, has always been bound by transport dimensions that had to be observed from the quarry to the building. Each of the three materials has its own inherently traditional local aspect. Faced with limited transport options, there was an advantage in proximity between the building site and the place where the materials were obtained and processed. This means that, almost inevitably, a local culture decisively shaped the face of places. The dark brick along Amsterdam's canals, rather small-scale when compared to its Central European counterpart, reflects a distinctive and characteristic chromaticity and scale, just as much as do the vivid, red sandstones of Glasgow's gridded streets or the robust, sunburnt fir wood of Alpine buildings.

Unlike concrete, these three materials have an integral component of scale that is directly linked to how they are processed and made, with their production. Concrete can be poured without any size restriction, thus concealing how it is made. It was not without reason that, even with the Brutalism of the 1960s, the formwork for concrete buildings was given a very 'close' scale by using roughly sawn planks that, besides having a small scale (plank size, wood grain) also reveal the production process of forming and casting. Modern formwork for exposed concrete allows this to be suppressed completely. The architecture of brick, stone or wood, by comparison, profits directly from the conditions of production, which are at best revealed and manifested in how the façade is

1 Caroline Voet, *Dom Hans van der Laan: Tomelilla*, Architectura & Natura Press, Amsterdam 2016, p. 29.

2 Dom Hans van der Laan, in a lecture in 's-Hertogenbosch, 1968 (Voet, 2016, p. 84).

articulated and in the tectonics of its assembly. If Ruskin's expectation "see if it looks as if it had been built by strong men; if it has the sort of roughness, and largeness, and nonchalance, mixed in places with the exquisite tenderness which seems always to be the sign-manual of the broad vision"[3] still remains valid today, then it does so in these direct opportunities to generate expression from the materials.

Crafting the drawing

What determines the quality of a hand-drawn plan? What differentiates it from a digitally generated drawing? Is it the slow process of working on a drawing, which initially lies in front of you as a blank sheet of paper that must be filled? It is a strenuous path that goes from laying out the first guide lines, which divide up the sheet of paper and later make the various relations tangible, to the final stroke, which must be perfect for it to appear precise. Once the drawing itself has been laid out, the building parts in section are then outlined and filled in, and lastly, the areas in elevation and their jointing patterns are added. It is a process of working in layers that are laid one upon the other to produce the complexity of the drawing step by step. The drawing produced by hand—particularly in large scale—must be constructed according to its own logic, almost like a real building. Thus the drawing helps us to understand the actual building that is depicted. Drawing by hand entails erasures and corrections, which—unlike undo and redo commands—inevitably leave traces. Traces that, however, at best enhance the depth of the drawing and can underscore the sharpness that is naturally desired with a vagueness that serves to increase one's perception of precision. A CAD drawing cannot contain any vagueness, thus making it a perfect aid for digital workflows. This is most succinctly evident when working with BIM, where the drawing no longer exists as an artefact, but at most as a mere portrayal of the digital model. Building integration modelling has dramatically heralded the end of the drawing and relies on the networked intelligence of many things that are supposed to work together. Thus the cumbersome character of the drawn plan would, at first glance, seem to be obsolete. But it remains unclear as to how architecture's expression can still be assessed in this supposedly perfect world. The handcrafted drawing is, after all, not merely a portrayal; it is indeed a key to understanding a building. The culture of drawing goes far beyond just basic representation, reflecting architecture in its fundamental essence.

The scale of the drawing

Scale places us as human beings in relation to the things that already exist or those we are designing. We use drawings, models or prototypes as tools for communicating between ourselves and the world. In this function as intermediary, the scale plays a very important role. Choosing the scale to be used at the communication level is crucial and represents a clear decision in favour of a specific perspective, in favour of a particular focus. It was therefore a matter of great importance for us to increase the drawing scale and the size of the drawings. The drawing's scale of 1:10 has the advantage that not only the detail can be explored but, thanks to the oversized drawing paper, the entire façade can be depicted and contemplated. The detail represents a focus within the drawing as a whole. The large drawing formats accommodate not only the accumulated knowledge of the small things, of how the building components are joined and how they come together, but also the presence of the entire building and how the parts relate to the whole. The same also applies to physically constructing prototypes and models at 1:1 scale. Here the body is addressed, and in a best-case scenario, in this way a part of the whole can establish a relationship to us, both close up and from a distance. Last but not least, producing large-scale drawings is physical work. It involves the body. The act of perception goes beyond just looking, and the body becomes integrated in the process by doing, by crafting. This is extraordinarily interesting for us: designing architecture is no longer understood as a purely intellectual activity, but is in this way given a reflexive, corporal dimension.

3 John Ruski, 'The Nature of Gothic', in: *Stones of Venice*, 1853.

Drawings 1:10

Stone	Brick	Wood
10–17.10.2015 Glasgow	12–15.03.2016 Amsterdam	8–10.10.2016 Vaduz

During three workshops in Glasgow, Amsterdam and Vaduz, students of the participating studios made 1:10 detail drawings of the façades of selected buildings. The analytic drawing stand for different building traditions: the building blocks of the grid of Glasgow's city centre entirely made of stone, the Amsterdam school's expressive brick façades or the urban vernacular of the traditional wooden buildings of the Städli Werdenberg in the Rhine valley near Liechtenstein. Large scale drawings were finally used in the design studios in order to transport the knowledge of the previous research phase into the project work of each student and to cultivate the power of hand drawing as a design tool.

The big drawings were essential in helping students to gain insight into the qualities of the façades and the used materials. We came to understand that working at a large scale echoed the difficulties of working with stone, brick and wood. In the process, we discovered the value of the drawing as a crafted object unmediated by the computer. The selection underlines the role of drawings as instruments of knowledge that fuse the conception and construction of buildings and offers a fundamental insight into the crafting of stone, brick or wooden façades *and* making a hand drawing.

Stone

A Analytic drawing
S Student project

A01 Brunswick Hotel:
Segio Dias
Itana Celic
Ewan Wotherspoon

A02 Hatrack Building:
Mick Madder
Sabine Makovec
Toby Lindo

A03 Mackintosh Building:
Eric Goldhoorn
Manuela Türtscher
Weng Yi Wong

A04 Grosvenor Building:
Erik Brusse
Janine Alge
Gabriela Wäger

A05 North British and Mercantile Building:
Pandelis Zarakovitis
Bastian Nenning
Siti Hannah Basalamah

A06 Grecian Chambers:
Joeri van Wijk
Milena Fischer
Jerome Wren

S01 Max Meijer
S02 Alexey Boev
S03 Manuela Türtscher
S04 Gian-Andrea Beer
S05 Rogier van den Brink
S06 Milena Fischer
S07 Itana Celic

A01

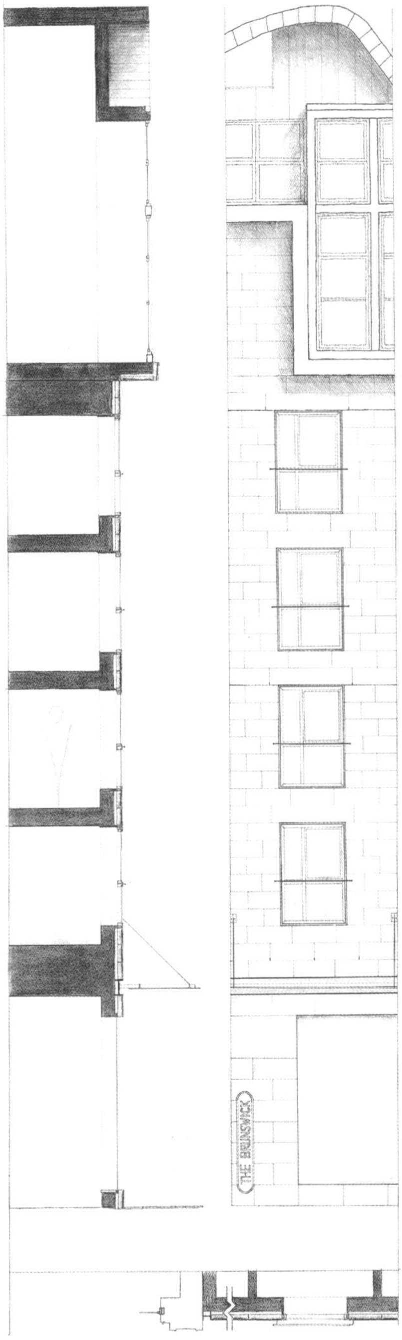

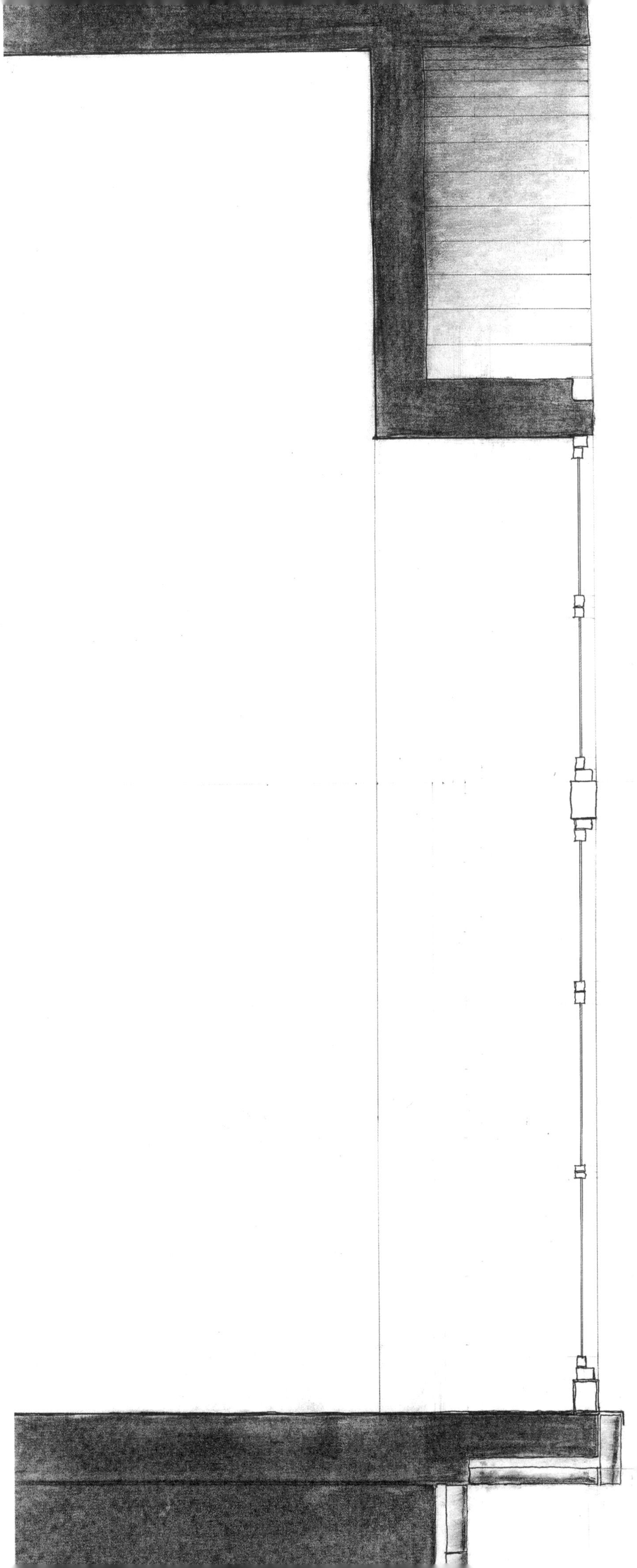

A02

A03

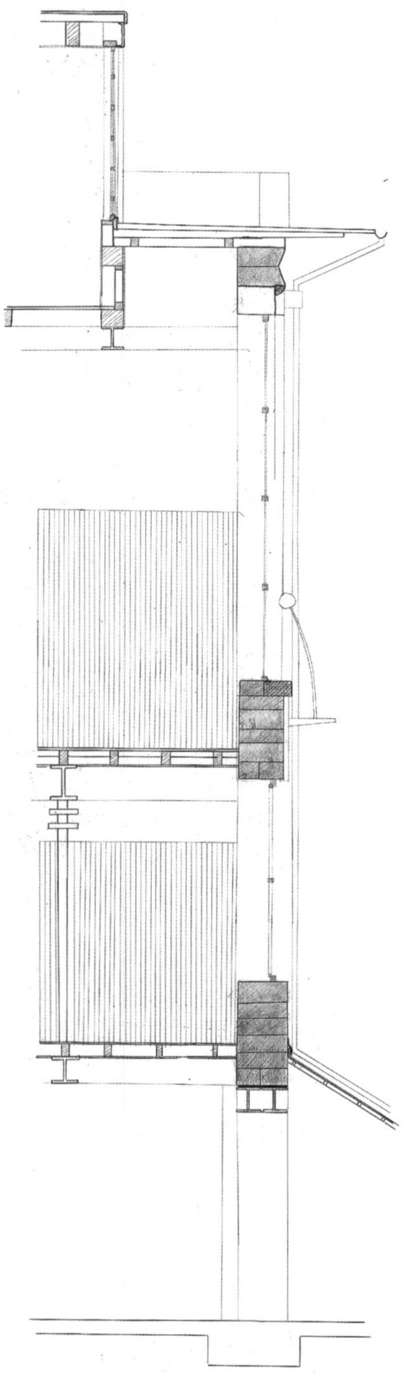

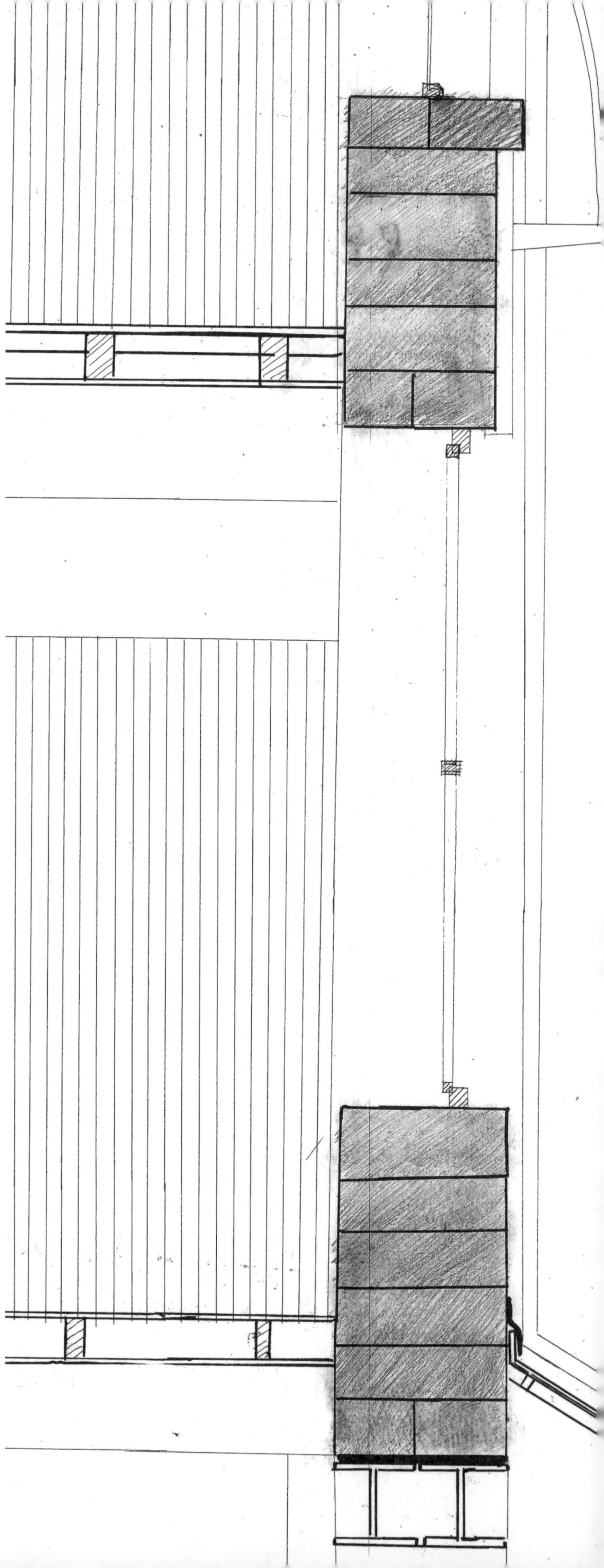

A04

A05

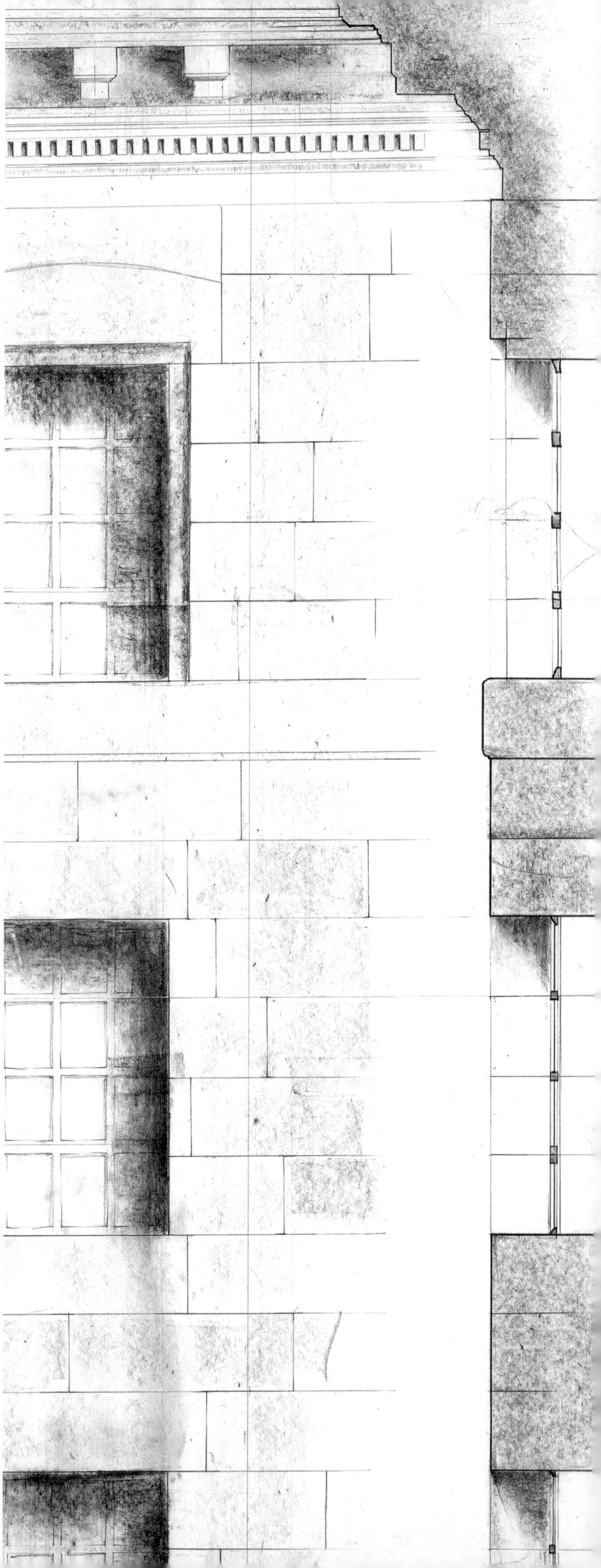

A06

S01

S02

S03

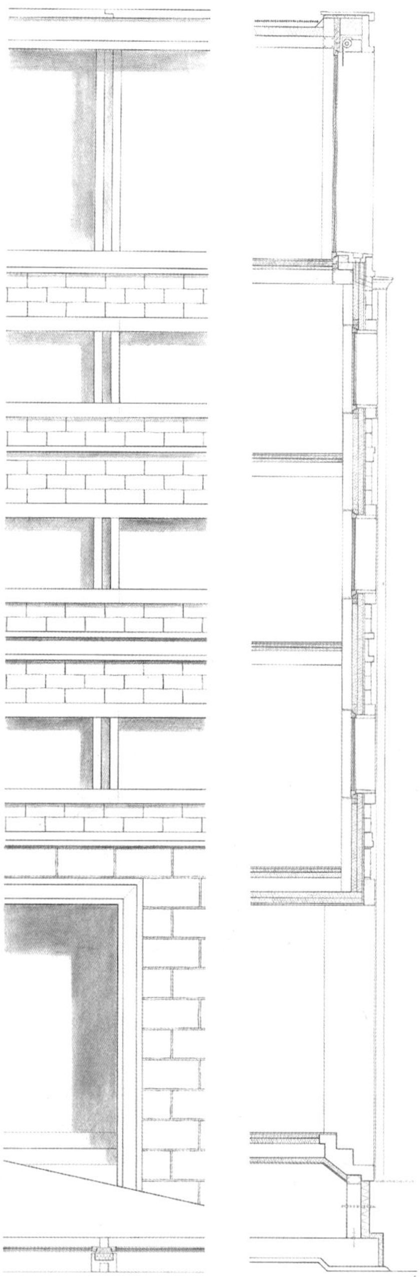

S04

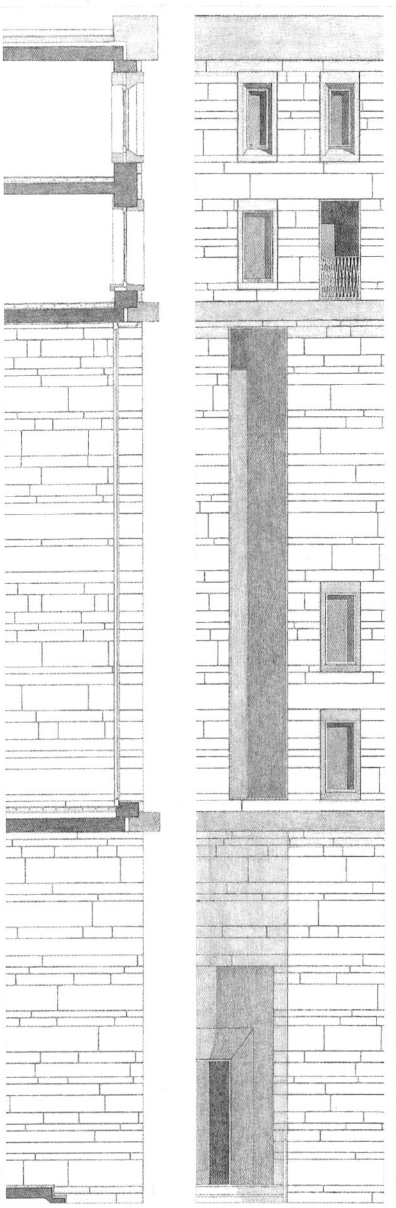

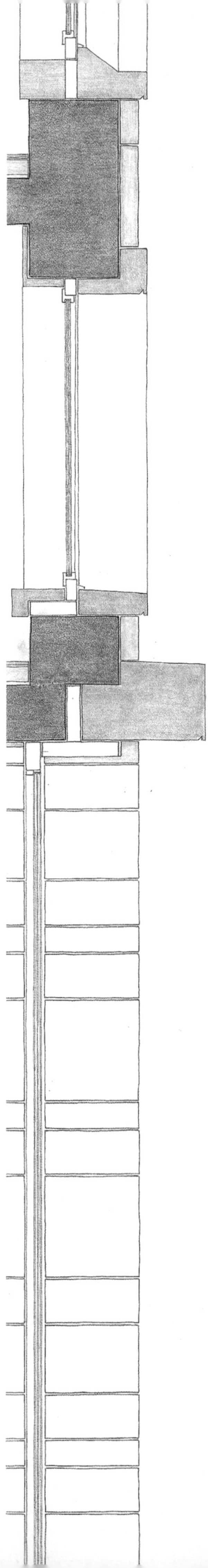

S05

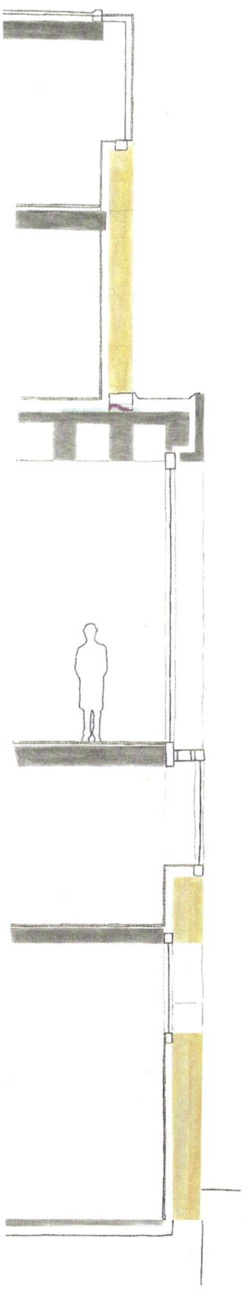

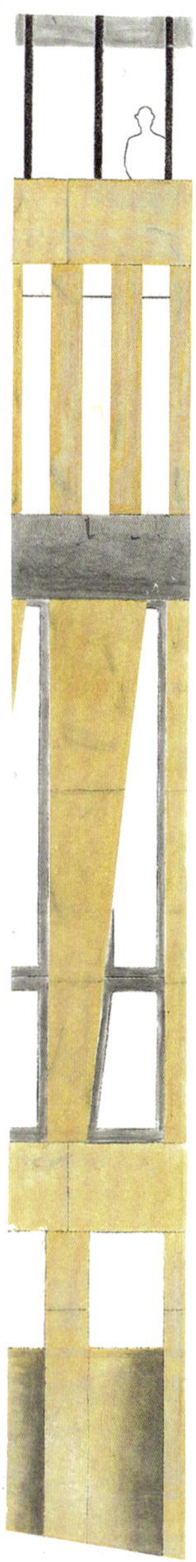

S06

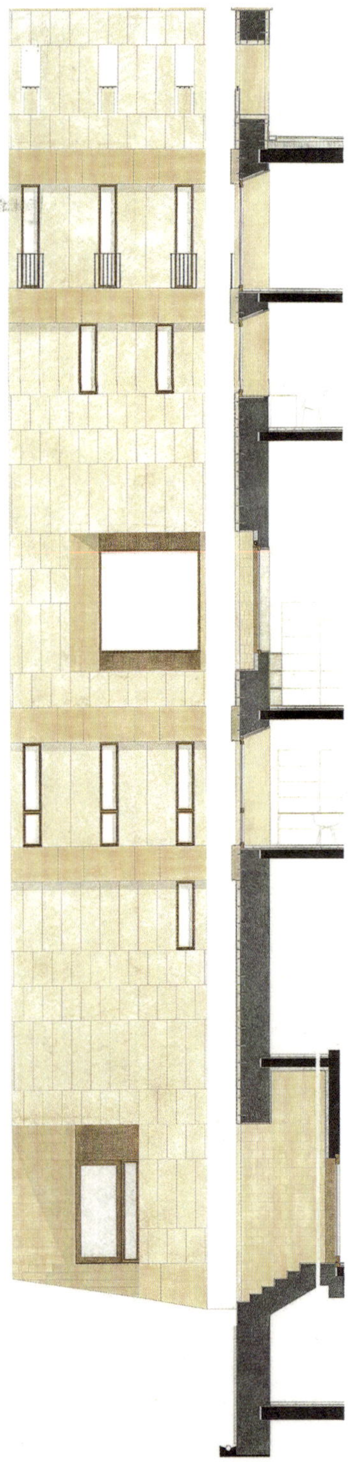

S07

Brick

A Analytic drawing
S Student project

A07 Loodsen:
Lucas Pissetti
Manuel Moser
Kirsty Shankland
Kristina Košić

A08 De Waag:
Andre Cramer
Brigitte Baier
Carl Baker
Lu Yu

A09 Coymanshuizen:
Thom Knubben
Viviane Göbel
Sandra McGrath

A10 Beurs:
Evie Lentjes
Shahanaz Hegazy
Bart van Pixteren
Jacco Pereboom

A11 Huis Bartolotti:
Juliette Gilson
Ewelina Langer
Matthew Healy

A12 Borneo Driehoek:
Stefan Koster
Christina Wieser
Brigit Luffingham
Fraser Stark

S08 Arne de Gans
S09 Viviane Göbel
S10 Manuel Moser
S11 Brigitte Baier
S12 Valerie Rainer
S13 Maximilian Kindle

A07

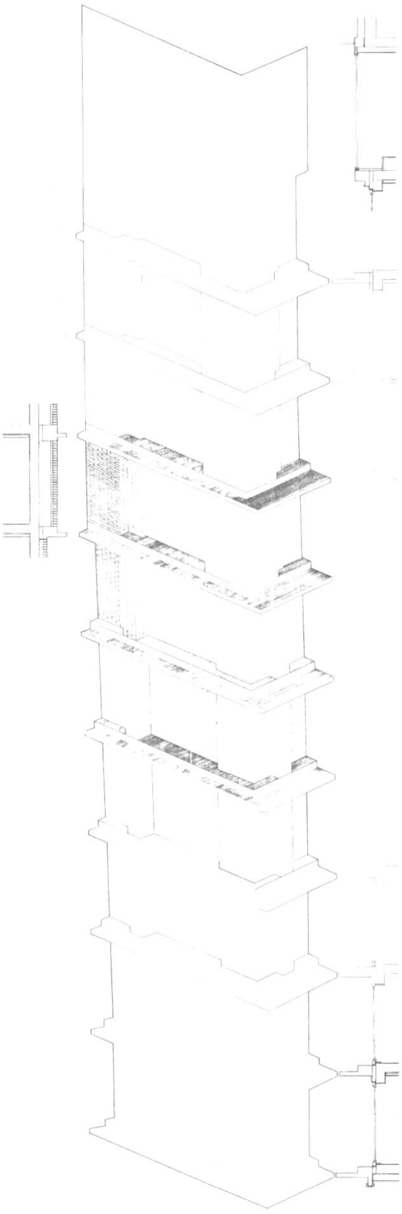

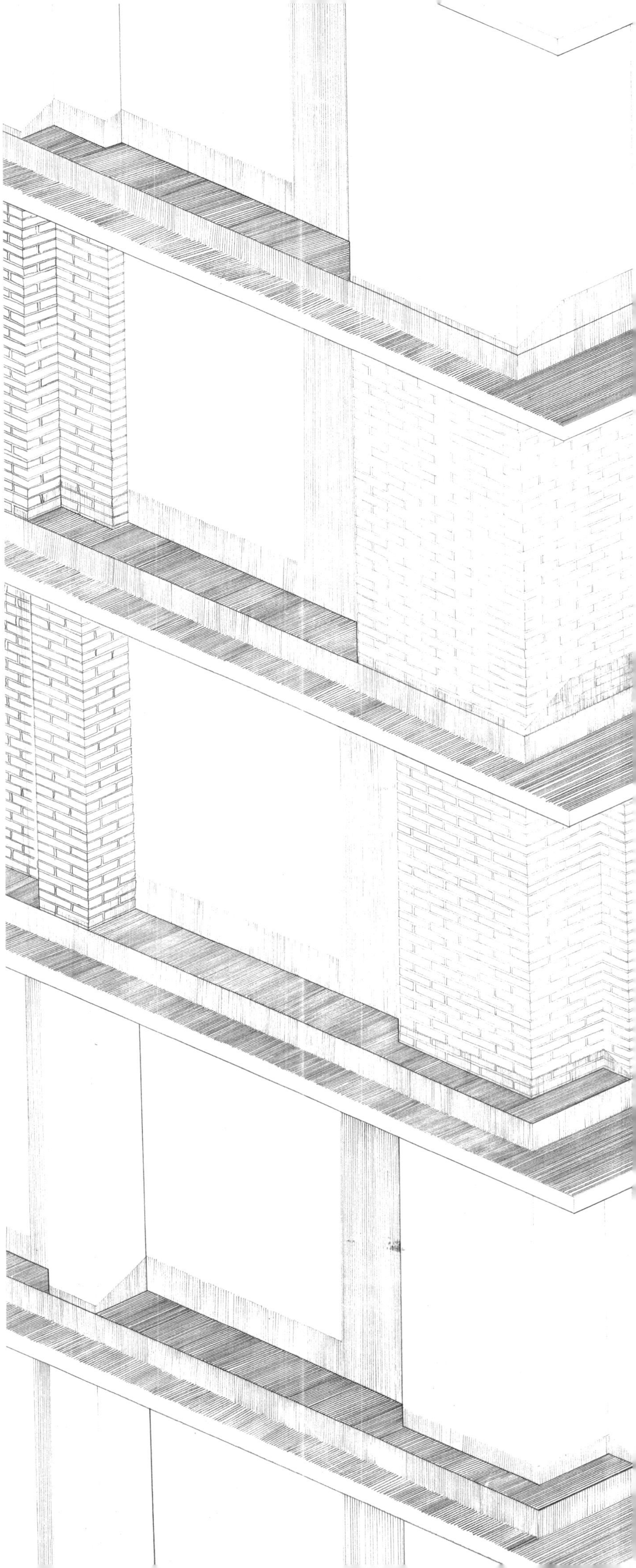

A08

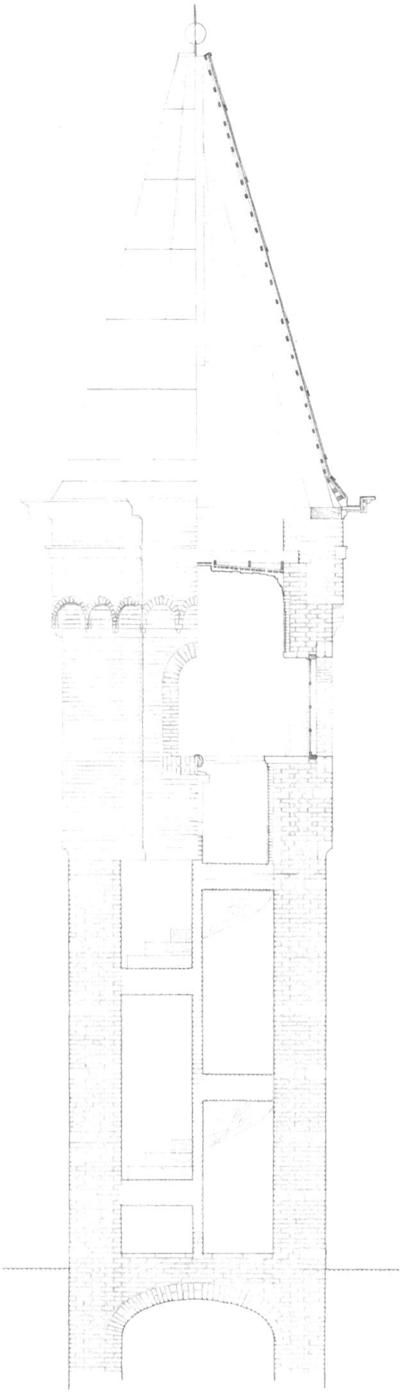

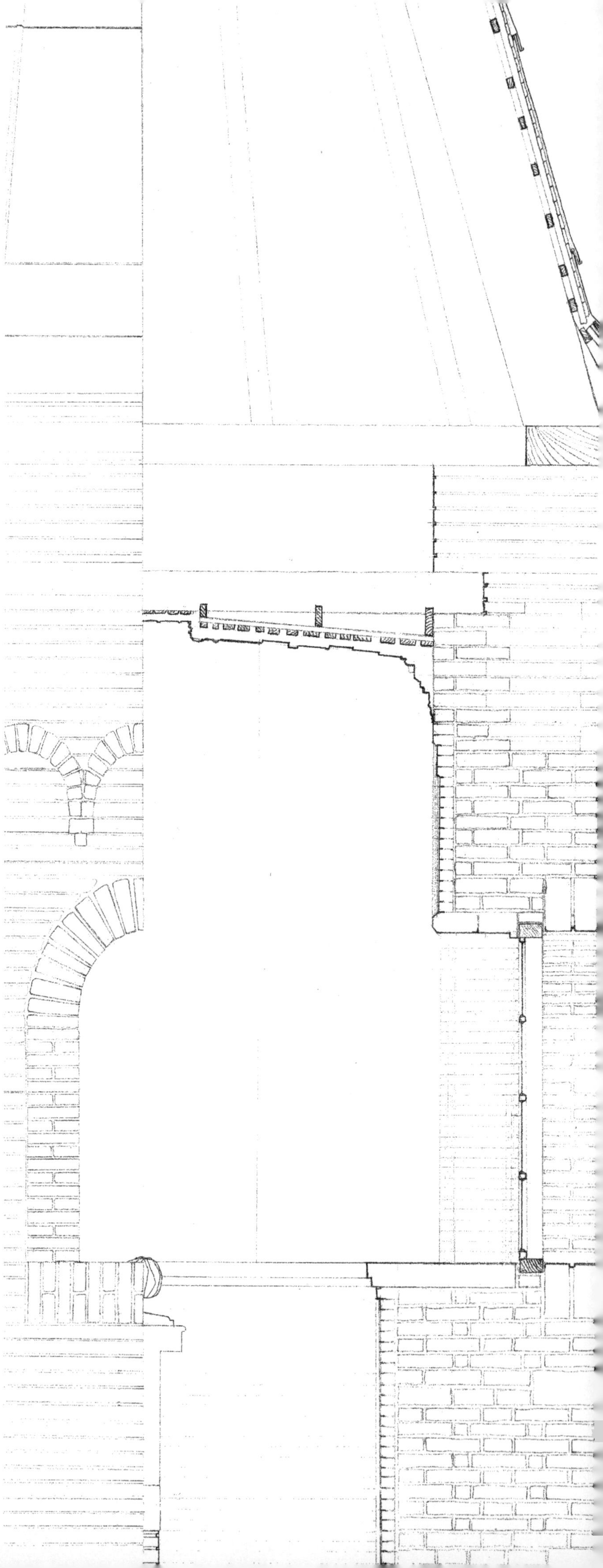

A09

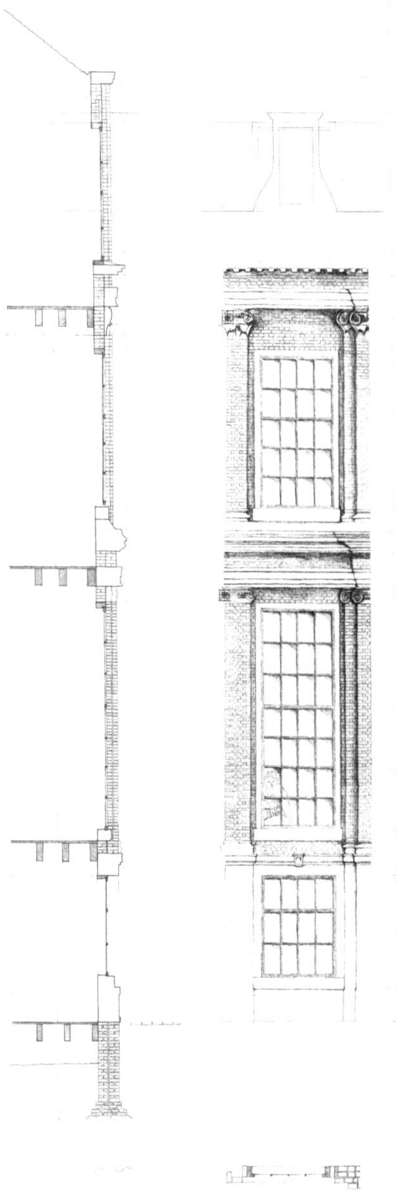

A10

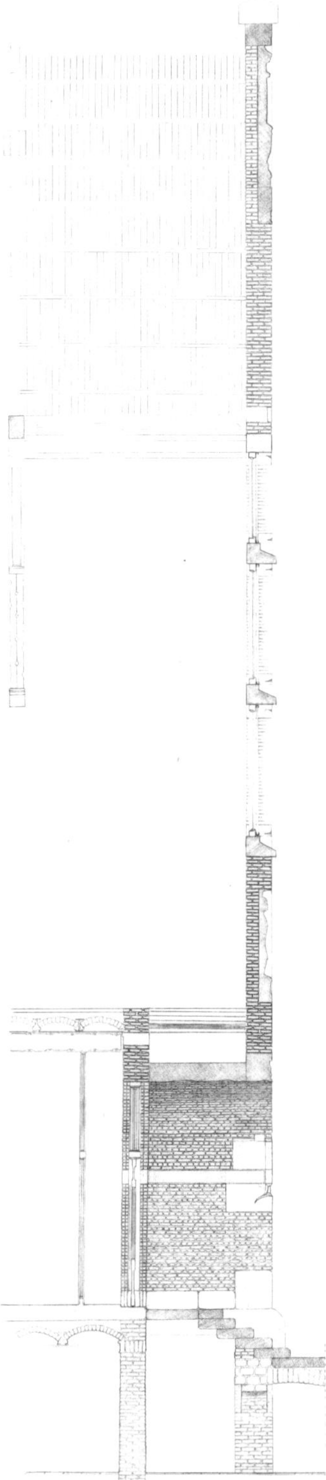

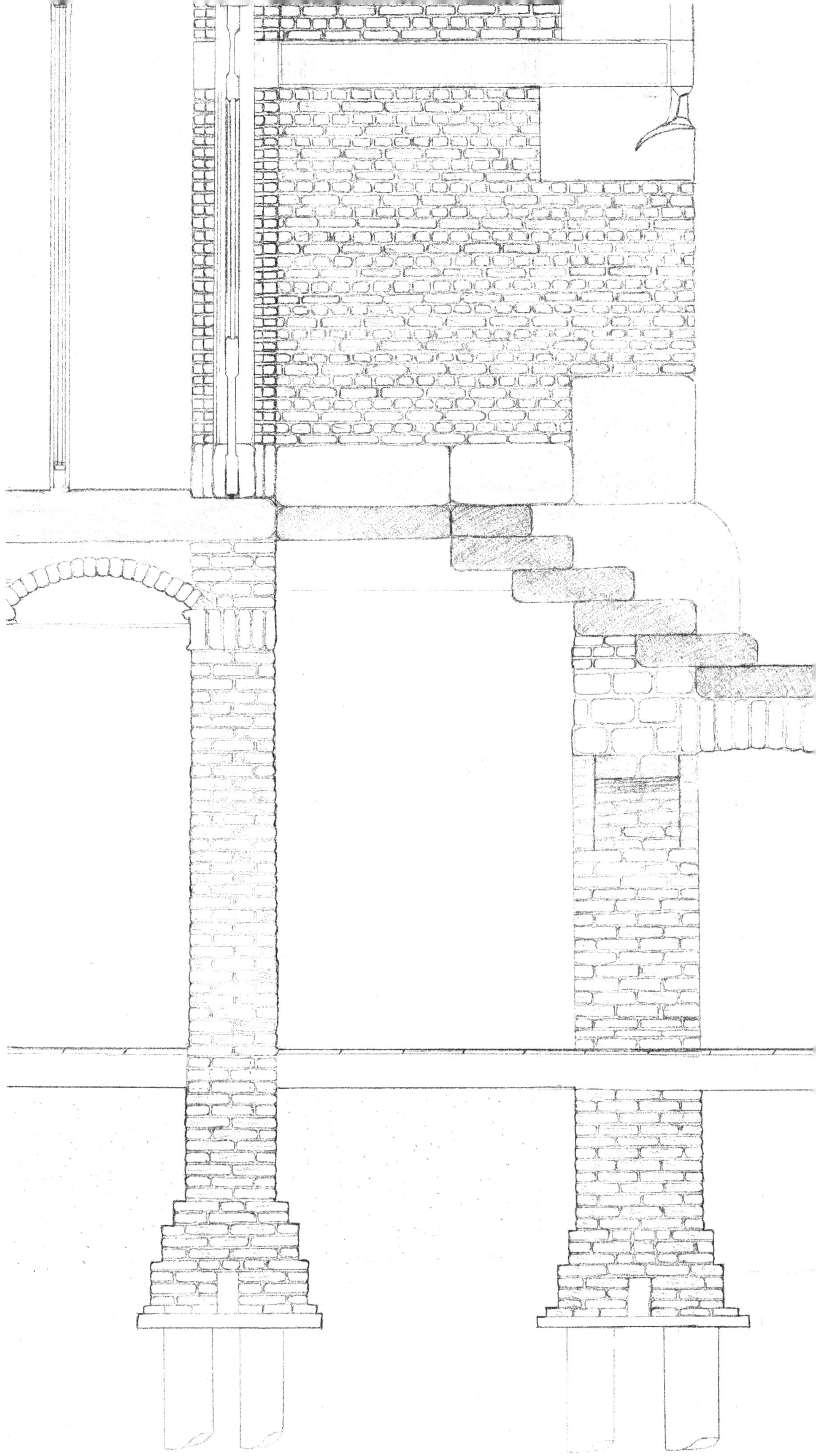

A11

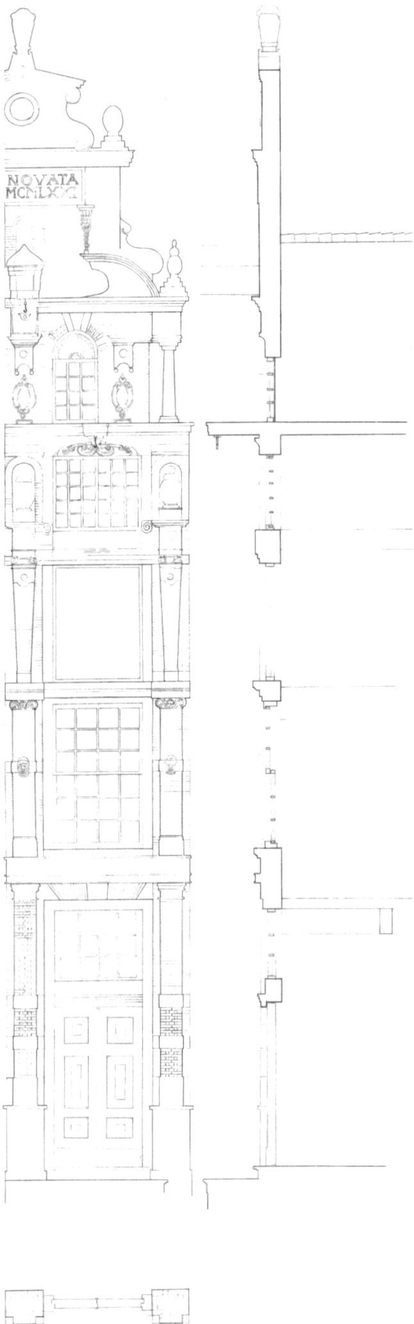

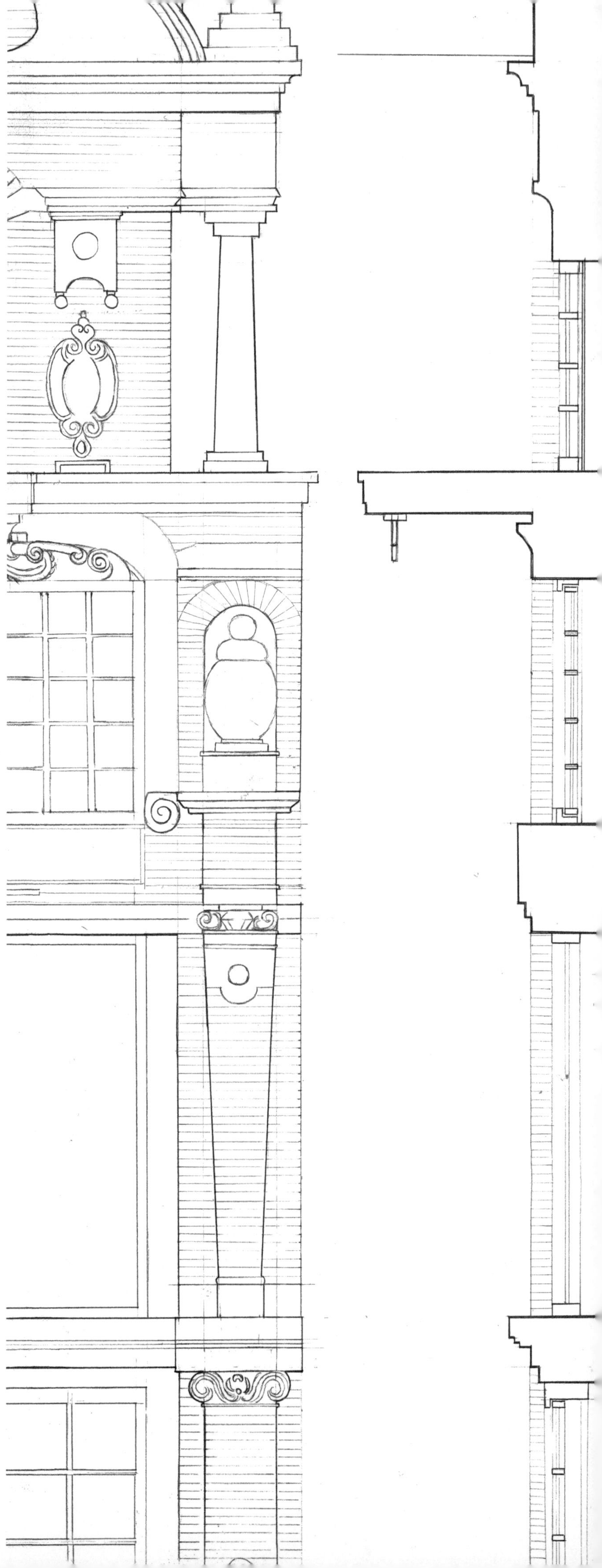

A12

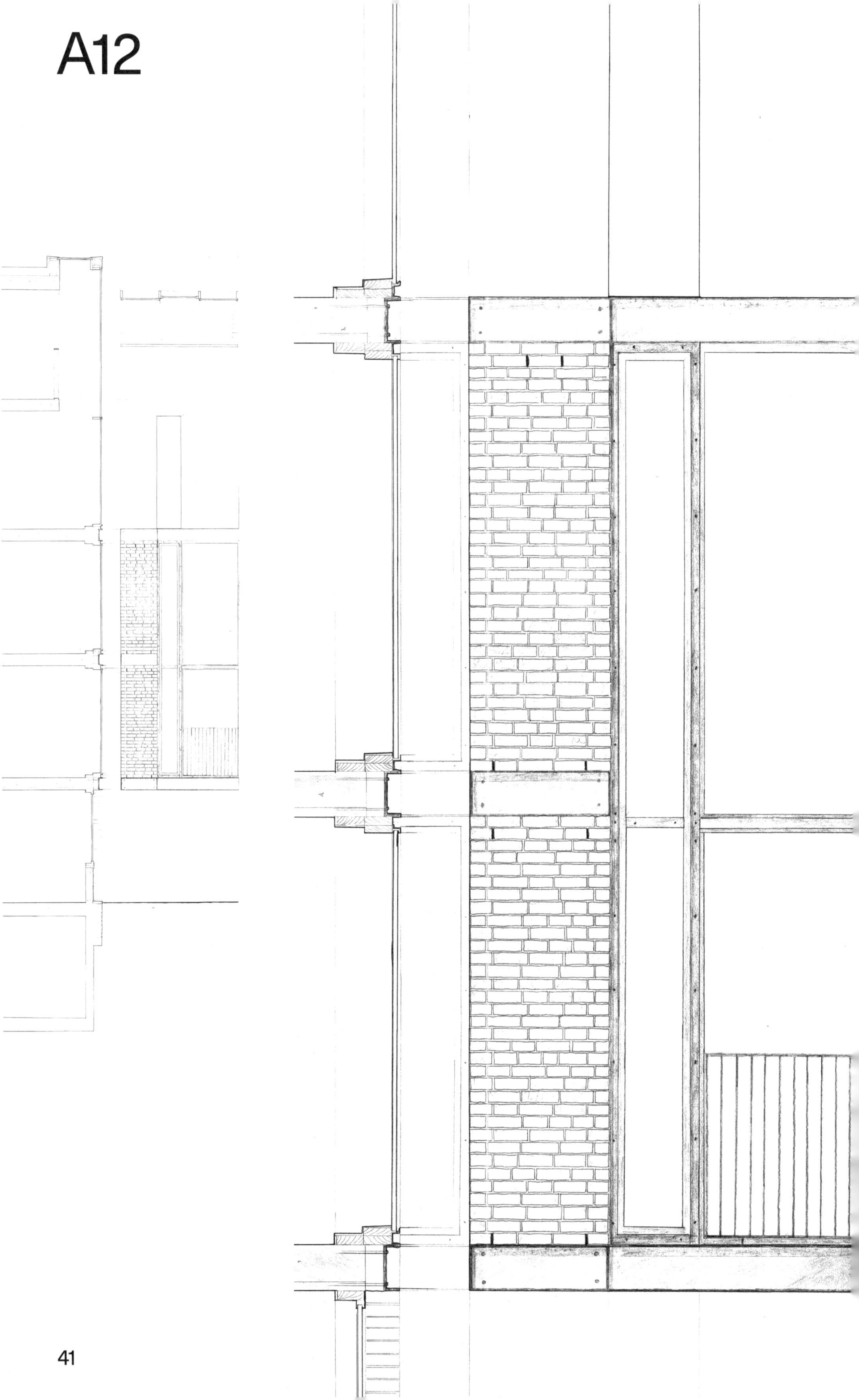

S08

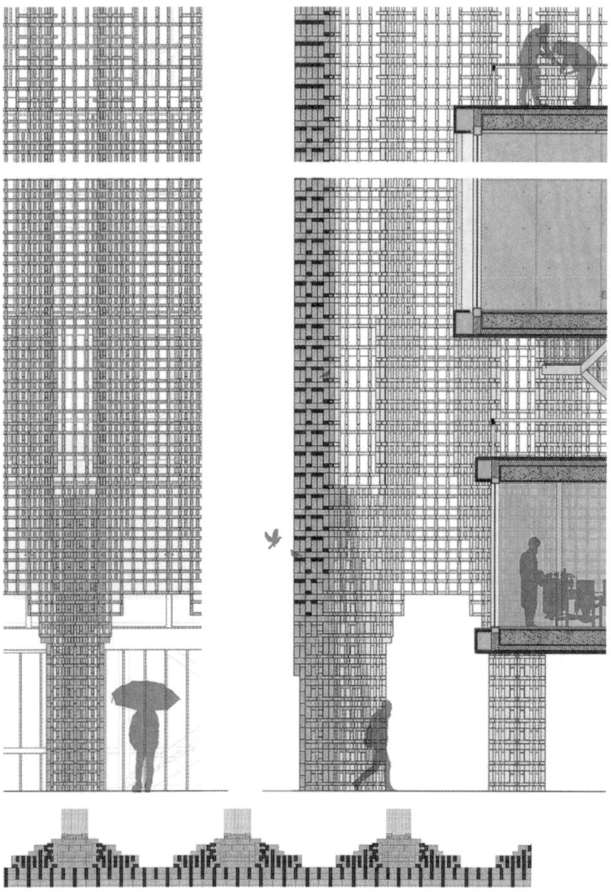

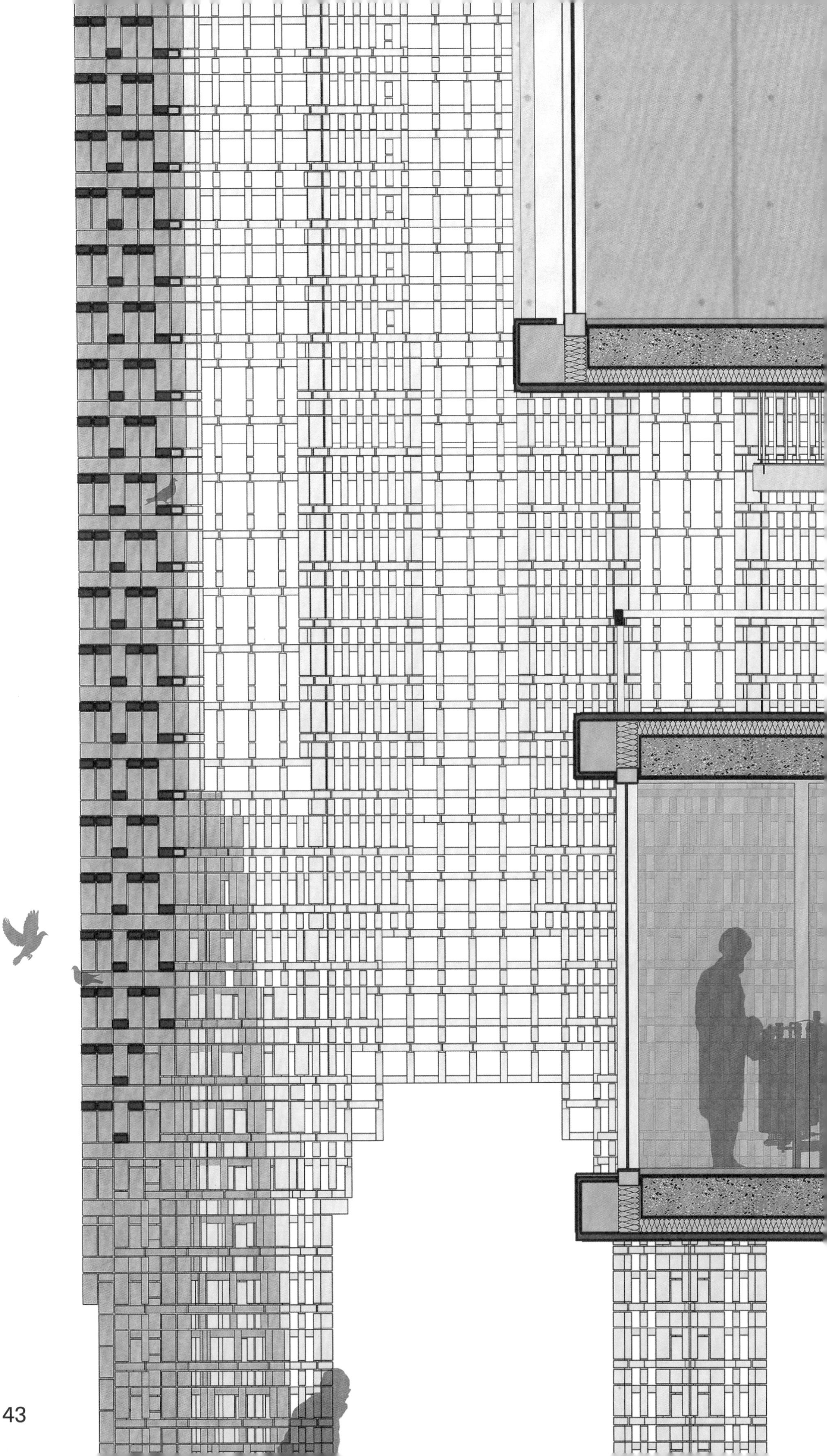

S09

S10

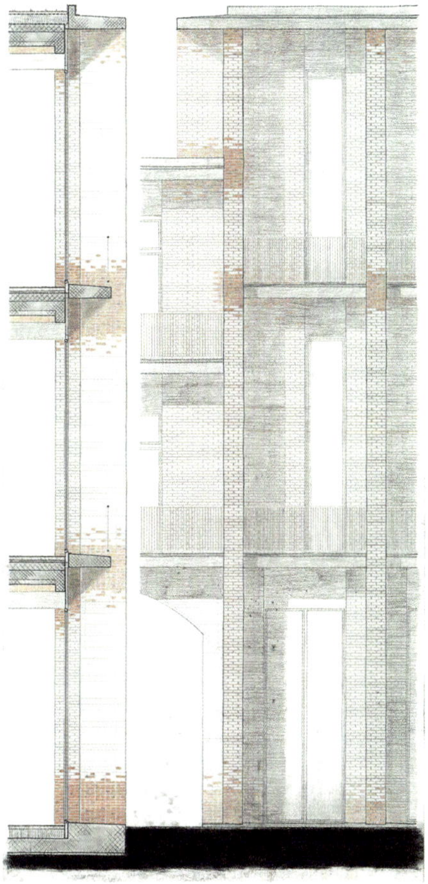

S11

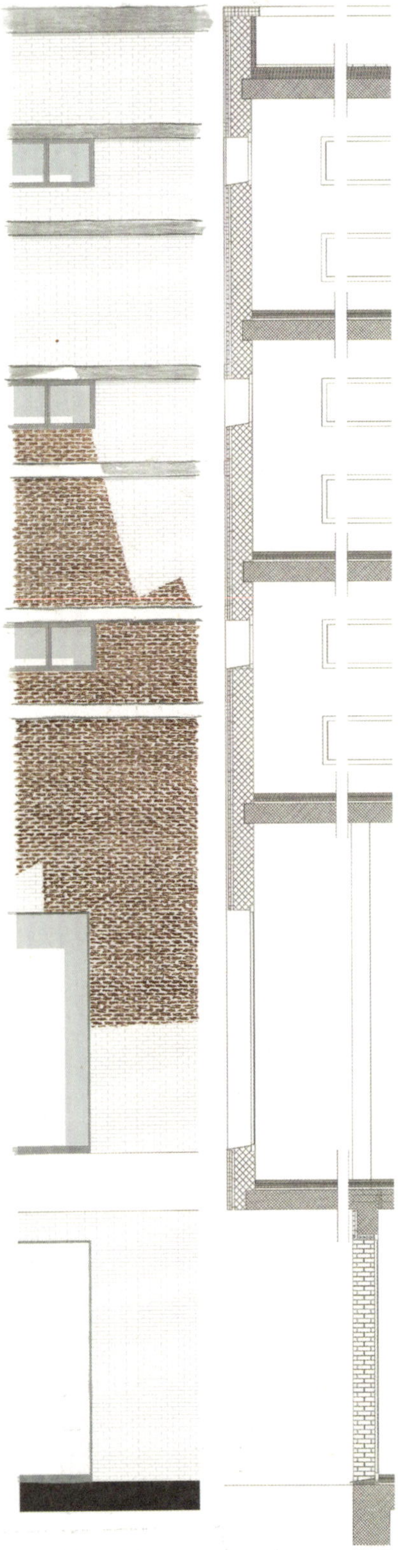

S12

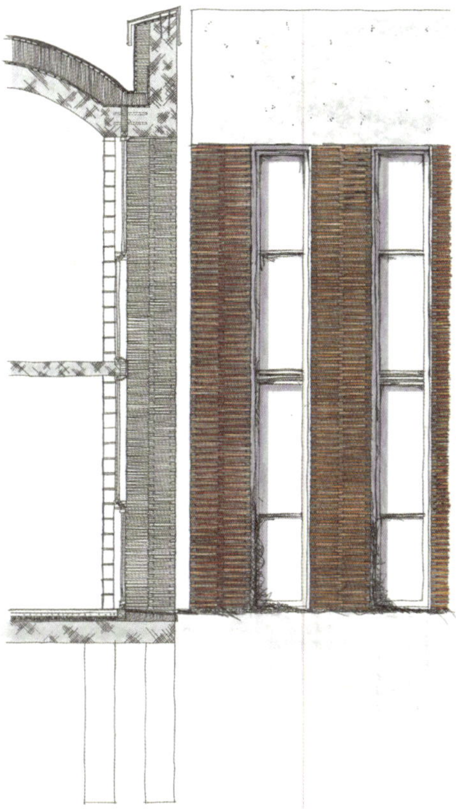

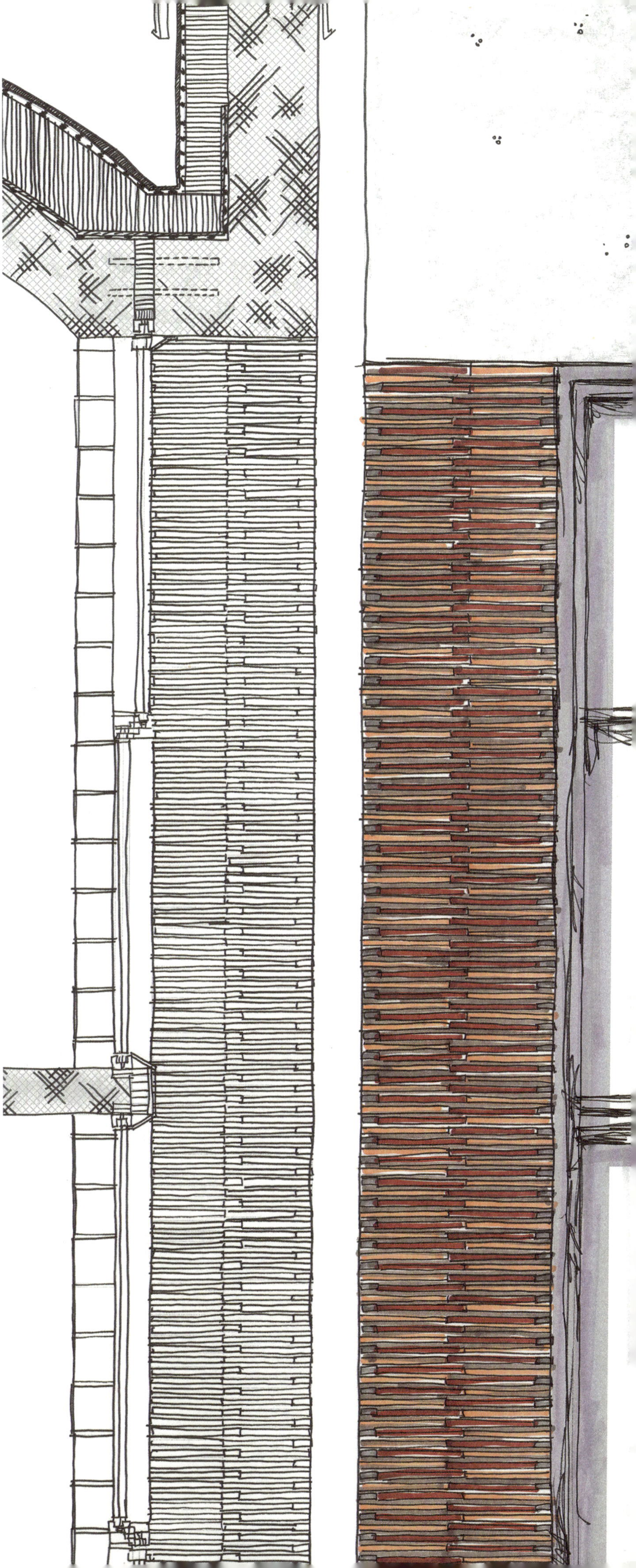

S13

Wood

A Analytic drawing
S Student project

A13 Begijnenhof:
Chris Aerts
Danielle Groenendijk
Thom Small
Sjef van der Sterren

A14 Schlangenhaus:
Julia Beck
Salaheddine Chekh Ibrahim
Ewan Hepburn
Eldrich Piqué

A15 Werdenberg Nr. 10:
Denise Pfleger
Paulien van der Valk
Pavandip Sian
Daniela Huber

A16 Werdenberg Nr. 23:
Julia Forrer
Midas van Boekel
Fredrik Frendin
Alexander Beeloo

S14 Dirk Overduin
S15 Philipp Althammer
S16 Tristen Vreugdenhil
S17 Anne-Lea Pfistner
S18 Simon Westreicher
S19 Nichole Samson
S20 Ries van der Bosch
S21 Midas van Boekel

A13

1888 1957

A14

A15

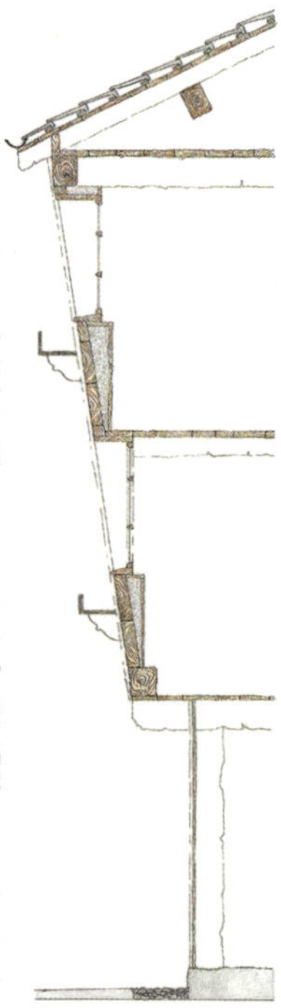

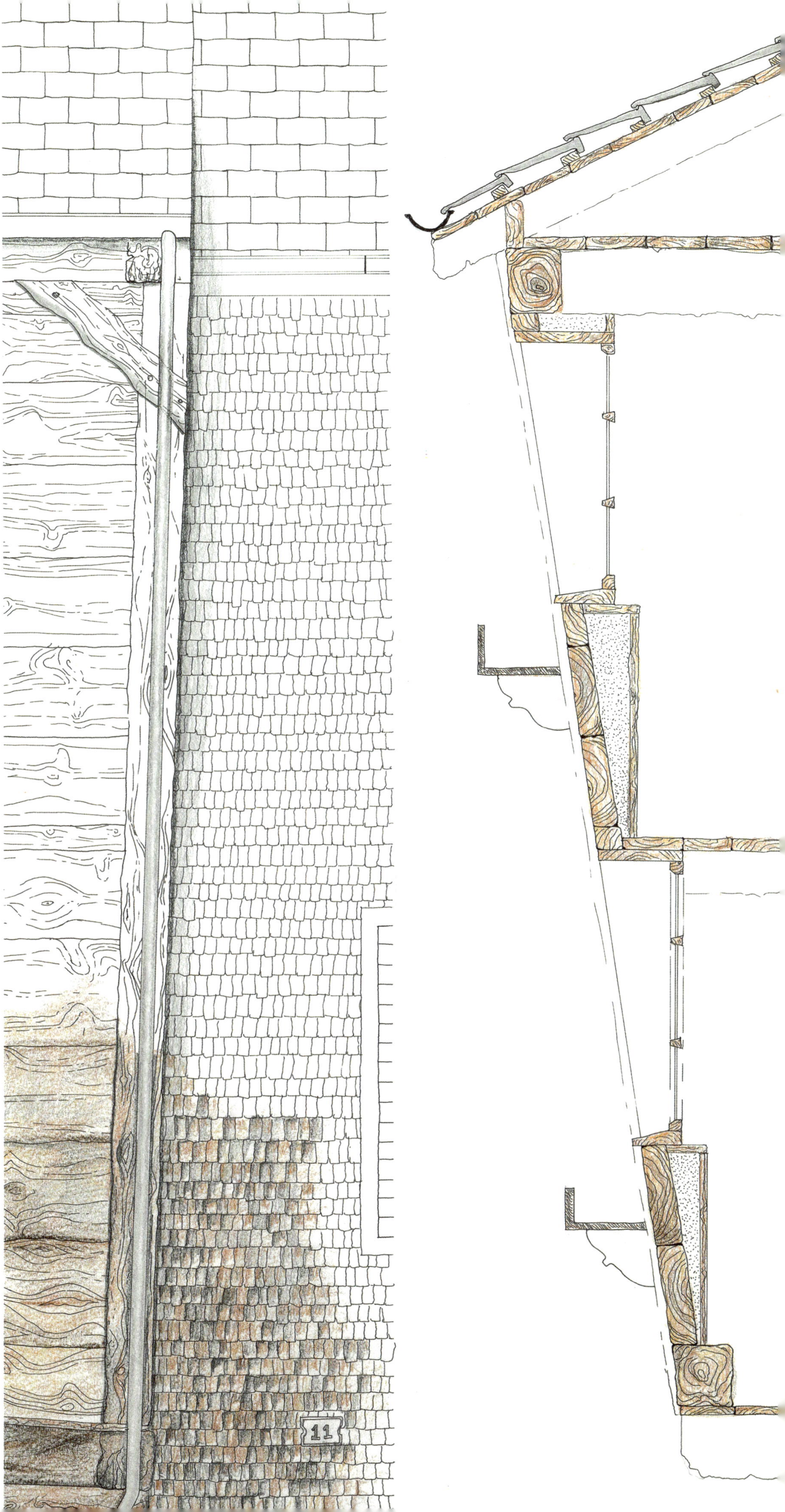
11

A16

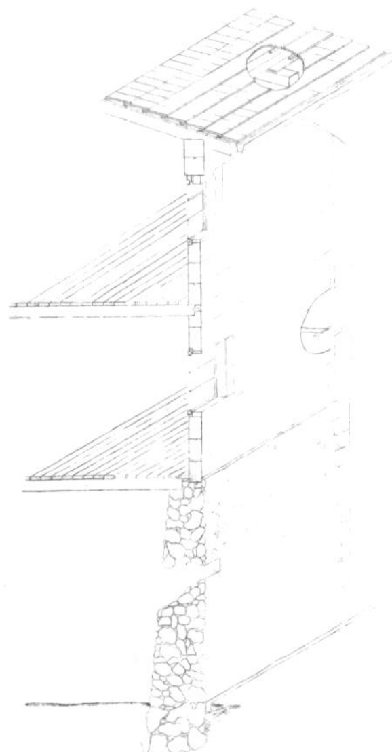

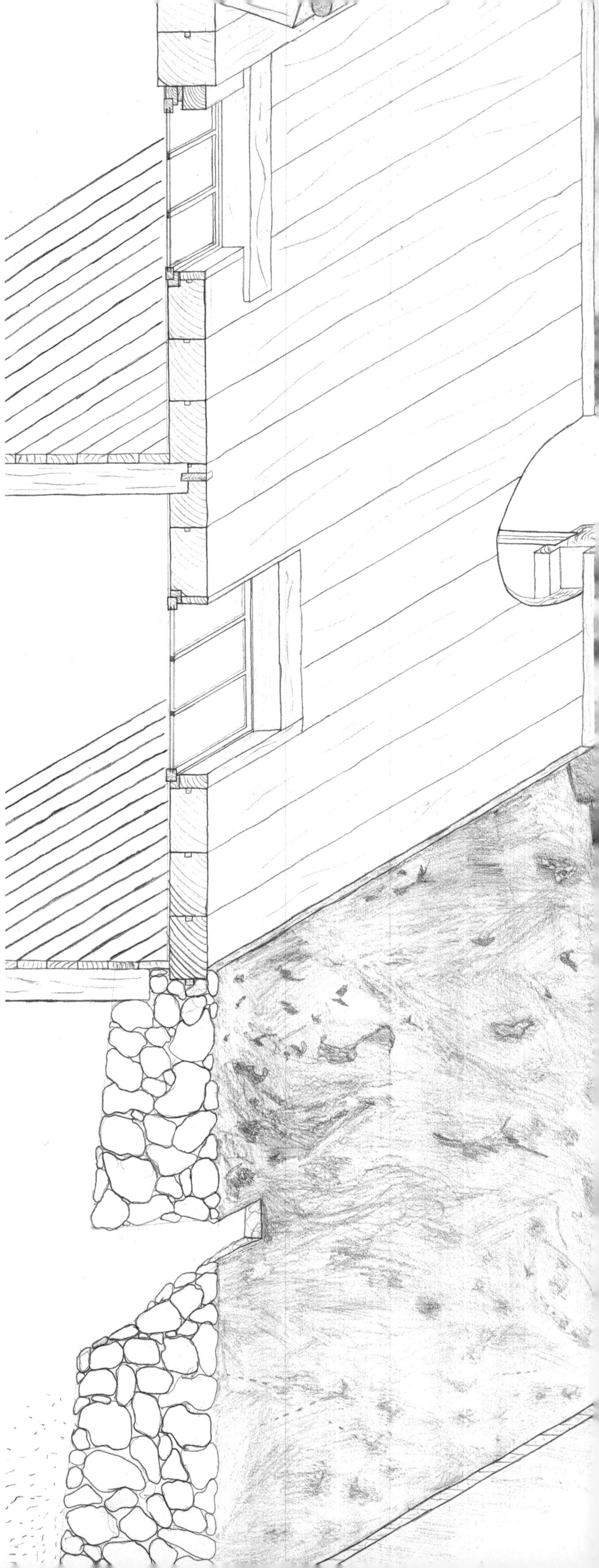

S14

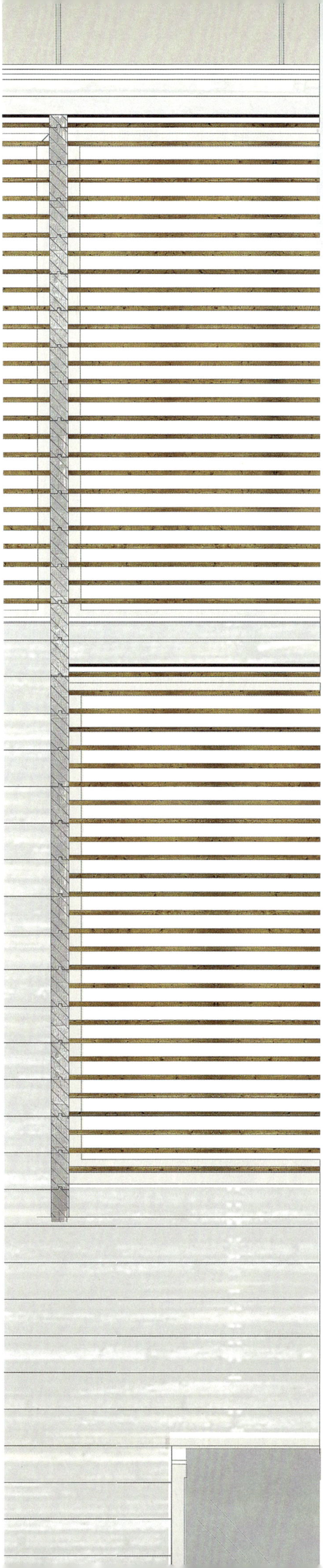

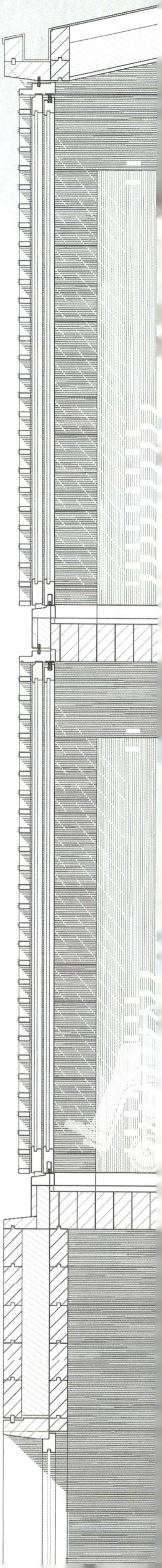

S15

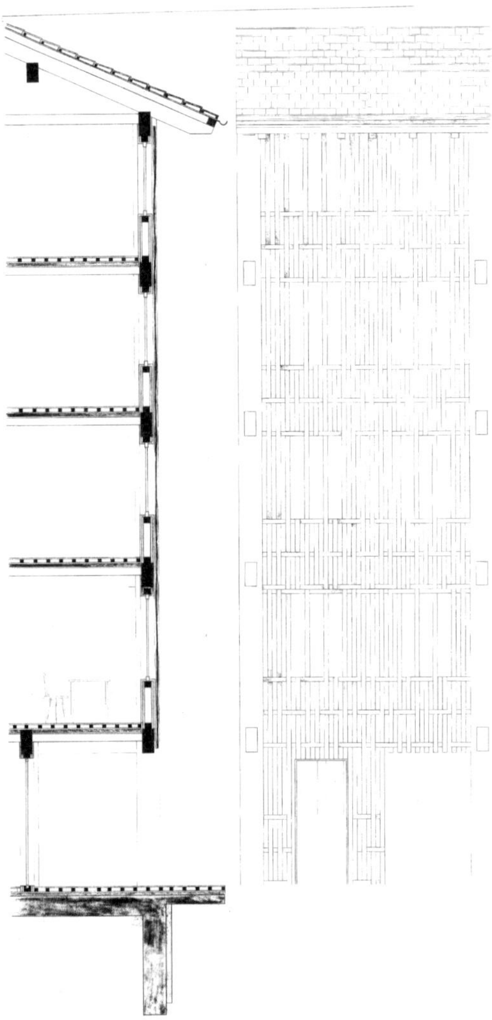

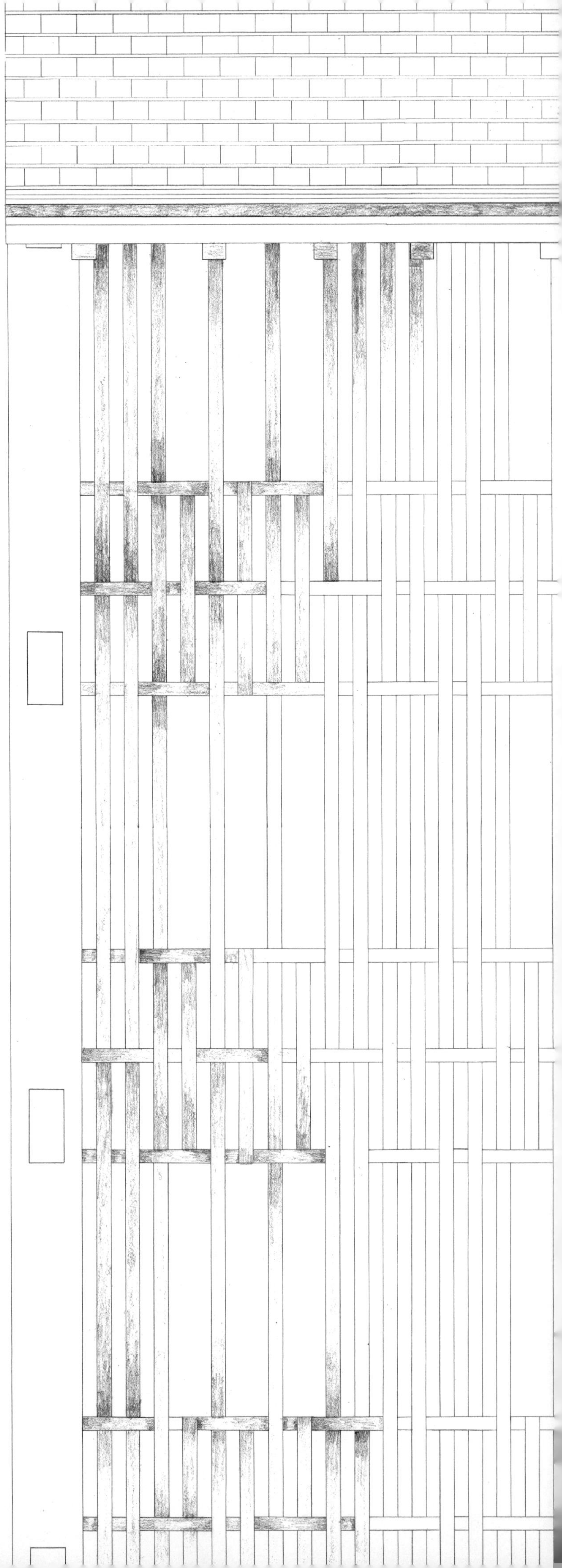

S16

S17

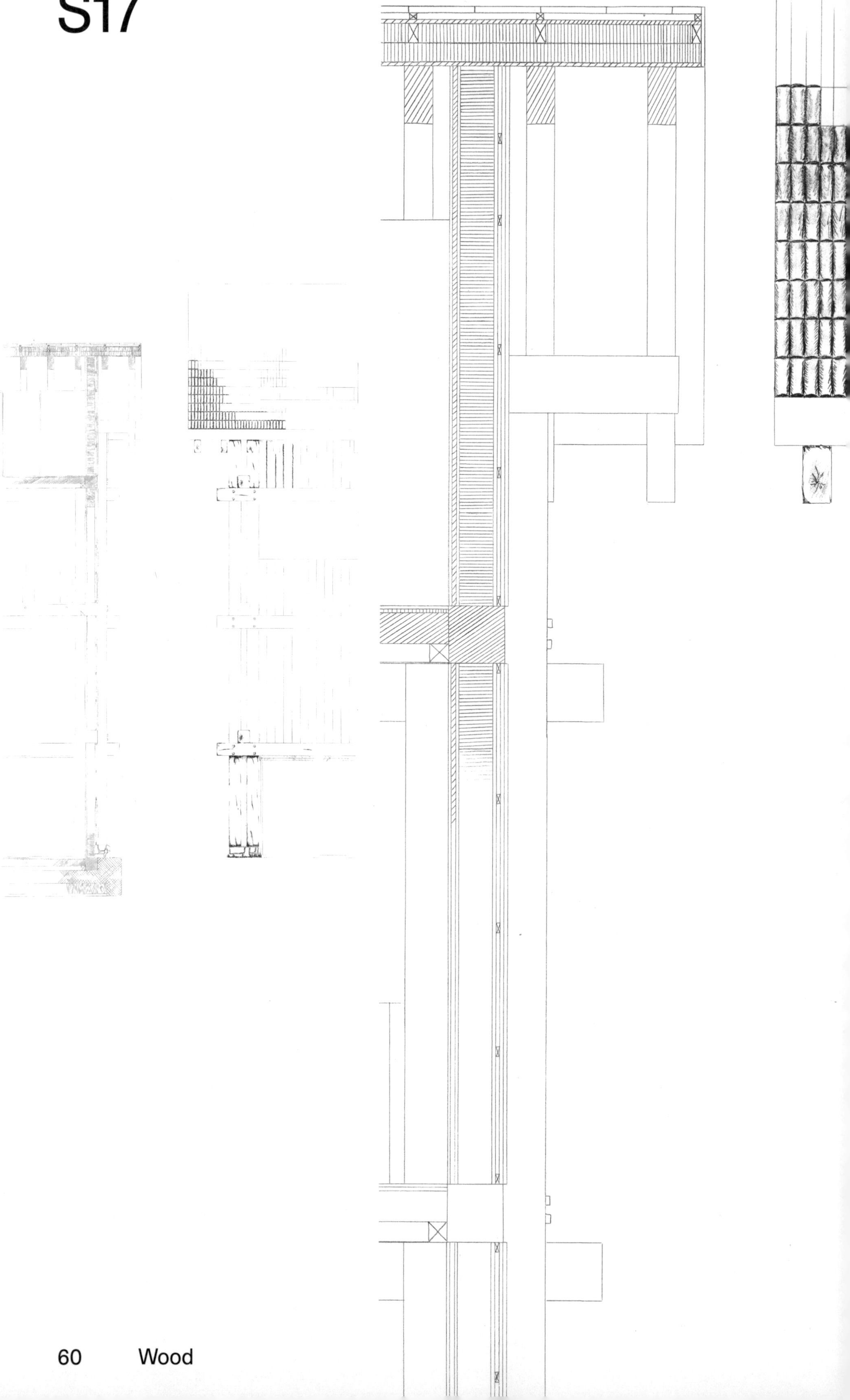

S18

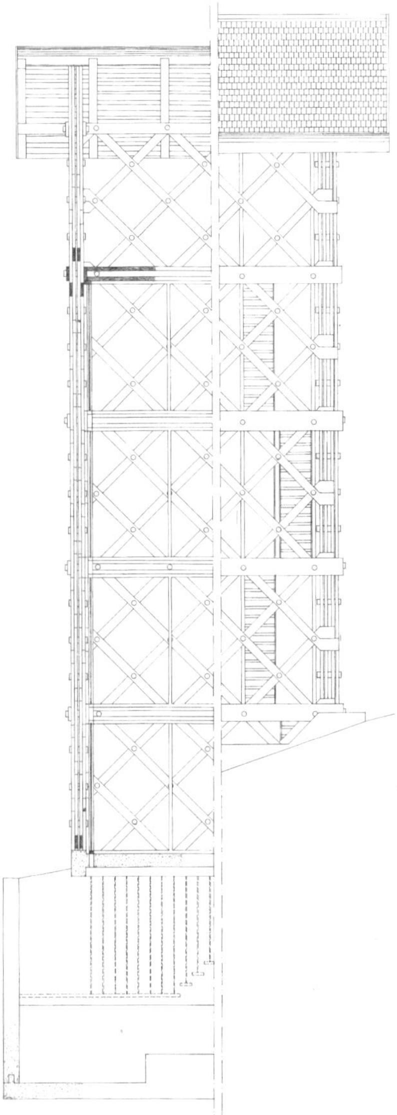

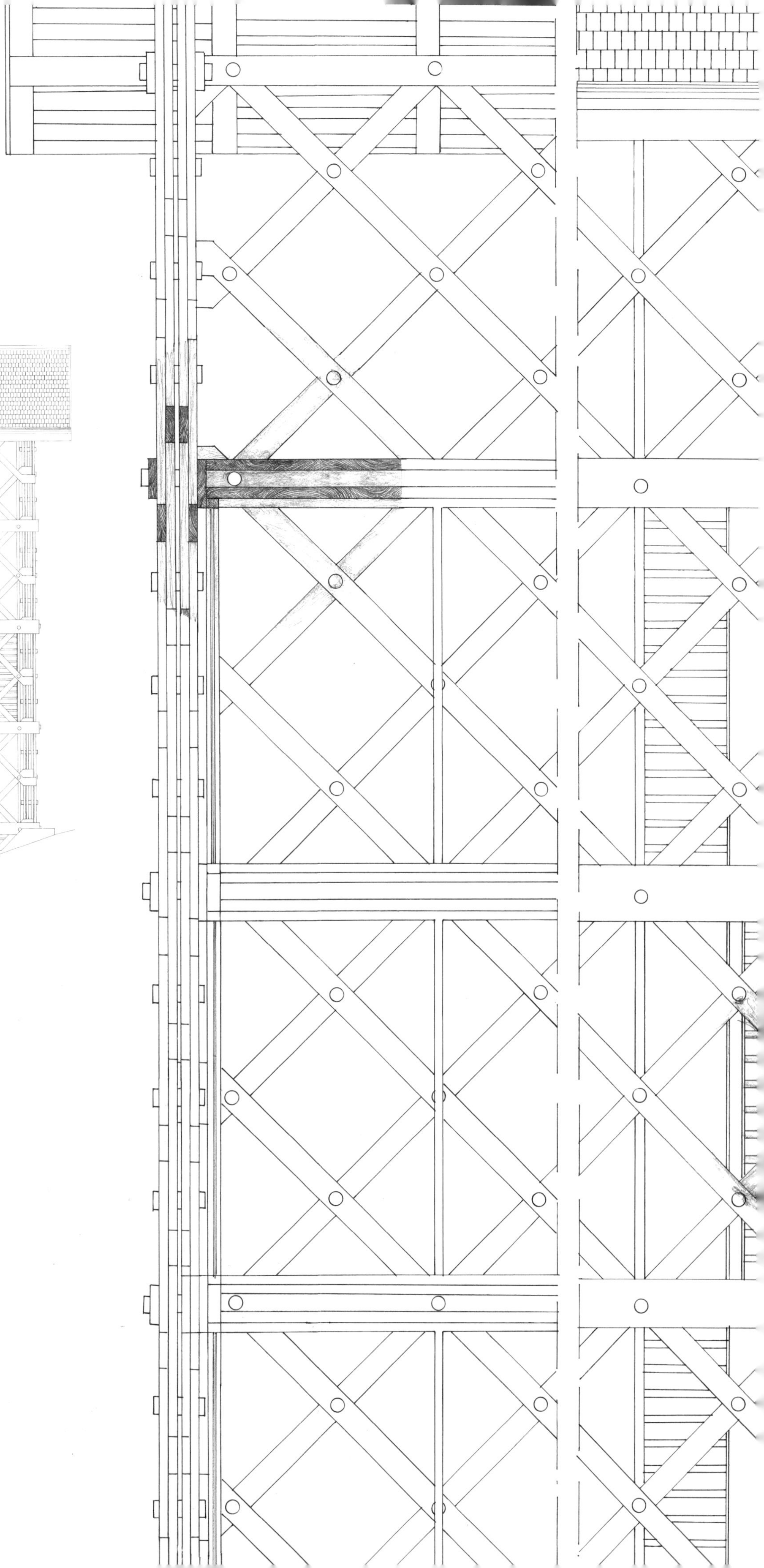

S19

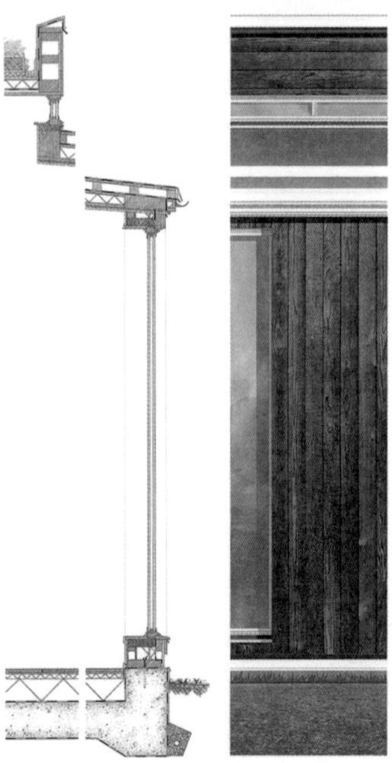

S20

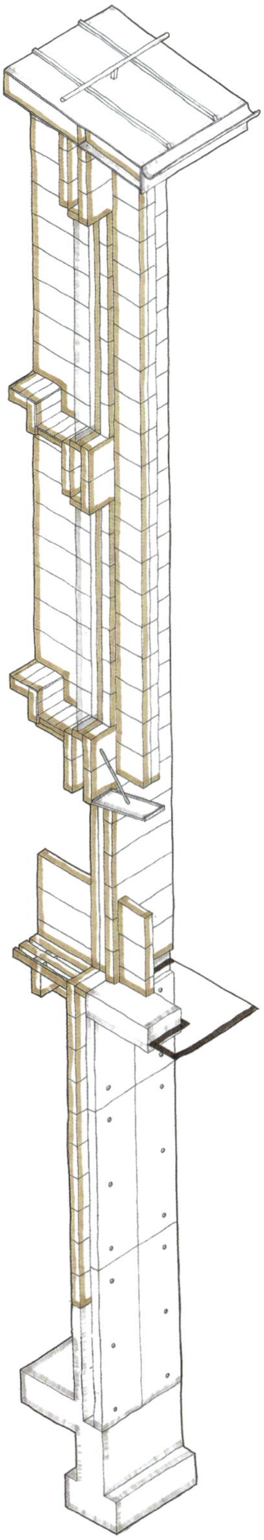

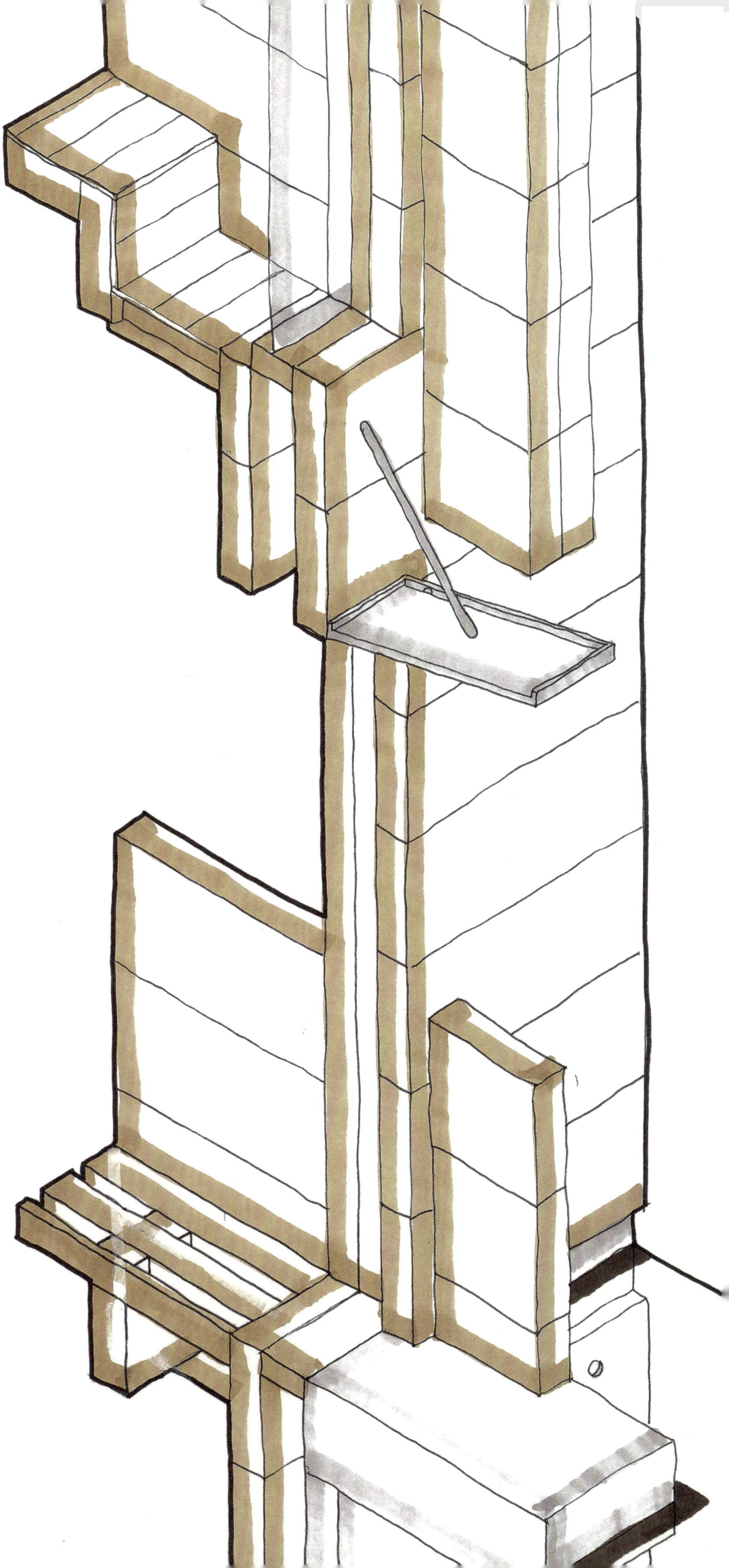

S21

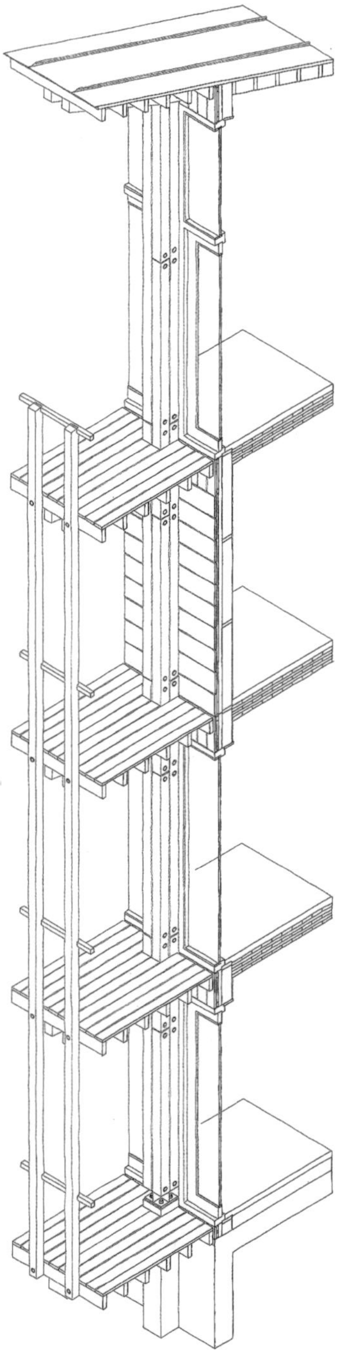

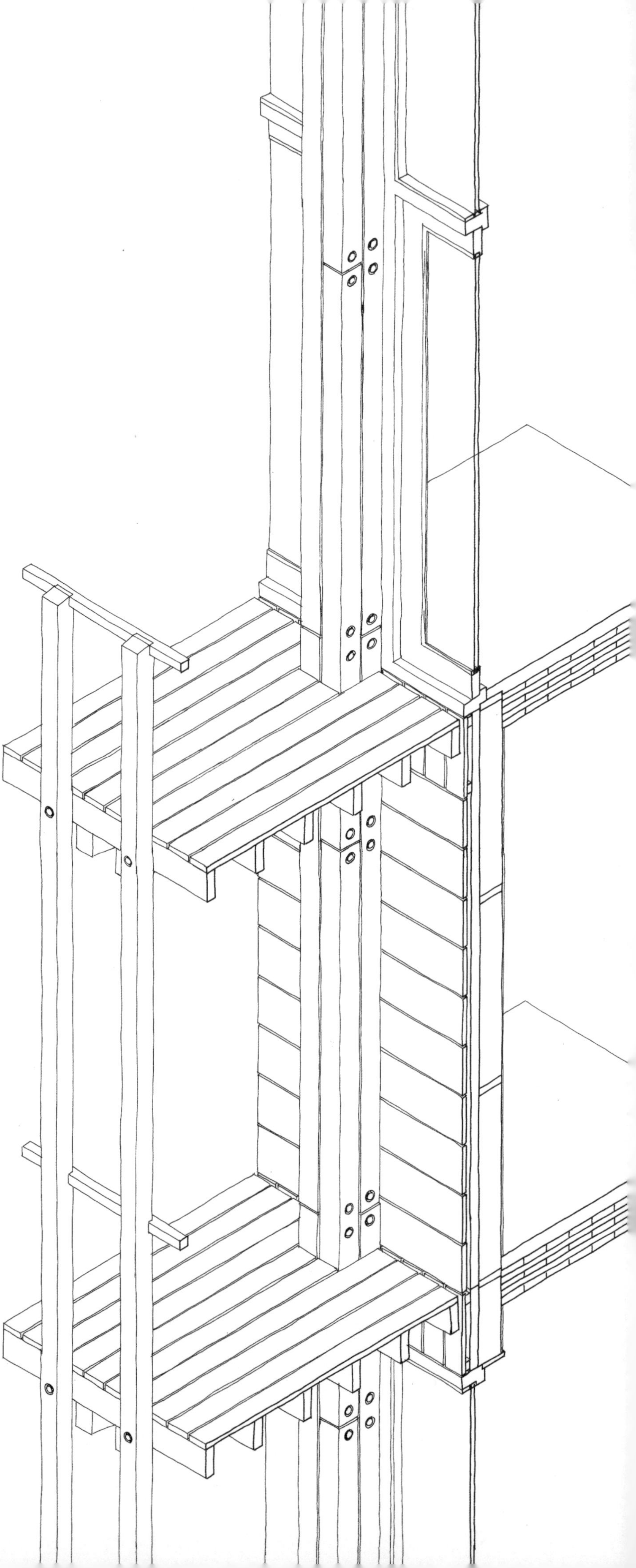

2 TECTONIC REFLECTION

Stone of Destiny

anald MacInnes

Can stone be political? In recent years Scotland has been in the grip of a mini crisis around the subject. The material has been desperately needed for conservation and also for building in heritage contexts. Quarrying and using stone in Scotland is widely seen as a necessary part of its make-up as a nation. Stone is the universal building material of the country, a 'differentiating factor' which gives it significance. For, as Gion Caminada remarked, 'difference is power'. By the 16th century Scotland's city streets were lined with stone buildings, and by the beginning of the 20th century the humblest of tenement dwellings had a stone front. In this way the ordinary buildings of the country followed the example of the astonishing architectural creations of the Stuart monarchy in the 15th and 16th centuries, which created monumental set pieces on a huge scale. The language of this triumphant architecture filtered down, first to the nobility, then to the middle classes of Edinburgh and Glasgow and beyond, and finally to the ordinary homes of the working class.

There are other materials of course, including many millions of bricks, but these historically have not been exposed in 'polite' buildings nor expected to convey cultural prestige. Historic timber buildings have all but disappeared. When the Edinburgh Old Town fire occurred in 2002, the event hit the headlines and we were deluged with messages of sympathy from foreign governments who had imagined a historic timber town reduced to ashes. In fact, the fire was localized and destroyed less than one percent of the Old Town, which is made entirely of stone. It is of course a nationalist trope to link the high and low culture across the social classes, but in this country stone is much more than a building material and seems to stand for a cultural and political position which we could call 'nationalist' in the sense that it seeks to assert localism or 'Scottishness'. It is not unusual for a building material, a song or even a dance (the tango in Argentina) to be brought into the service of cultural nationalism, but there is a strong and quite remarkable paradox here.

While stone has been a badge of the national it has also, simultaneously, denoted the *international*, which in Scotland has been no less than a plea for the right to exist as an independent culture. In a typically contradictory way, often misunderstood, Scotland has wished to be independent so that it can belong to an international cultural community. In a celebrated stunt on Christmas Day in 1950 the 'stone of destiny', on which the ancient Scottish kings had been crowned, was kidnapped by four nationalist students. The stone had been stolen by Edward 1 of England as spoils of war in 1296 and placed below the seat of the English throne in Westminster Abbey. It was soon recovered, but in a bizarre ceremony of repatriation it was brought back to Scotland in 1996 and given a place of honour at Edinburgh Castle. The sight of a piece of red sandstone, carried in a converted vehicle reminiscent of the 'pope-mobile' being cheered through the streets of Edinburgh was strange indeed.

Scotland, perhaps more than any other country, has a stone culture. In this sense the comparative cultural aspect of the Erasmus programme is very interesting. Brick and wood are important cultural signifiers in the Netherlands and Switzerland respectively. That much was clear from the programme and from the presentations and discussions in Liechtenstein. Stone in Scotland is, however, on a whole different level of cultural significance. In 1998 I was verbally attacked during a lecture. I had been talking about a new building in Edinburgh's famous Royal Mile, designed by the arch-stone traditionalist, Ian Begg, for the Scandic Crown Hotel in 1999. The building was 'wallpapered' with historicist rubble, wilfully asymmetrical windows, and has a gigantic corner tower, worthy of the 16th Stewart monarchy. One critic was outraged at my showcasing this blatant piece of 'Disney-fication'. Another thought that anything other than load-bearing stone, properly laid, was not 'traditional'. The building had the honour of being slammed by modernists and traditionalists! That is the cultural power in Scotland of stone building. For many years and until fairly recently, Glasgow City Council would not allow brick or rendered housing. In the 1930s the city pioneered factory-made artificial stone for council houses when stone itself had become too expensive. The reputation of the city as a progressive place, beautifully built, was at risk. In Aberdeen, granite buildings could not be demolished without special permission. The 'Silver City' was made by and with granite, since its vast quarries were the city's main source of wealth.

This is all very heady stuff and it is worth saying that the heat has gone out of the argument in recent years. This is largely because stone as a building material in Scotland has regained its prestige for heritage contexts and prestige projects, not in a rhetorical, 'nationalist' manner but with respect to context and place-making. In one sense, buildings in Scotland are either stone or not stone, but beautifully engineered concrete has become a kind of stone substitute because of its monumentality. Meanwhile, new stone in small, handle-able, module sizes offers the right material on the wrong scale. Concrete offers 'monumentality without rhetoric' but an abiding notion in Scotland holds that prestige buildings need to be made of stone. What being 'made of' something actually involves is another matter. It remains controversial simply to hang stone from a steel or concrete structure or to import massive concrete panels already faced with the material. On the other hand, there is little doubt that the material has been reinvented in Scotland and that the 'narrative' of stone building has been exposed as a myth, allowing the material to 'speak the language' of the present and not the past.

Brick is the Medium. The Façade is the Message

dira van 't Klooster

On how construction material can convey political ambitions

Construction materials in façades can be important message-bearers. An ample use of marble communicates wealth, which is why bankers favour this material in their headquarters. High-tech materials can psychologically be linked to innovative strategies, which is why construction companies and ICT companies like them. Solid stone assures the public that villains will remain inside the prison walls. And glass façades transmit the notion of political transparency in town halls. But these messages to communicate status or intended use can hardly be called political. At the Erasmus+ Symposium 'Crafting the Façade: Reuse, Reinvent, Reactivate' in May 2017, students from three architecture schools around Europe researched and developed façade constructions made from three materials prevalent in local building tradition and culture—stone (Glasgow), brick (Amsterdam) and wood (Liechtenstein). While emphasis lay, obviously, on aspects of materiality, students also focused on the cultural and political aspects of construction materials, or on how tectonics and materials can also support social change. Some examples from the use of brick in the 20th century in the Netherlands contributed to this awareness.

In the early 20th century in Amsterdam, national housing policy coincided with ambitious housing associations that advocated high-quality housing for the working class (Housing Act, 1902). The same happened in Germany and England, but never on the same scale and never with the same strong involvement and commitment from public bodies. Moreover, the Housing Act enabled housing associations and municipalities to use it as an instrument for urban planning. The Amsterdam School movement, which came about because of highly committed architects, housing associations and politicians, was not only an enormous improvement on the quality of large-scale social housing in Amsterdam, it was also the start of new ideas in town planning. Within the context of 'Crafting the Façade', the most interesting aspect of this movement is that the brick façades of the Amsterdam School became the message par excellence to convey the policy of elevating the working class by providing new, clean and spacious housing, and most of all innovative and elaborate detailing. In the façades of Spaarndammerbuurt or Amsterdam-Zuid, bricks are laid horizontally and vertically, and carved into all sorts of embellishing details, just as they were in the most expensive villas that were designed by the same architects at the same time. The Amsterdam movement was supported over a period of thirty years by the housing associations and the city of Amsterdam, and some 180 architects contributed to it, though maybe its most important achievement was the emancipation of the working class.

Social housing, city planning and bricks have since remained connected for a long time in the Netherlands and elsewhere, but a new highlight of Dutch public ambitions in brick façades was the Piraeus building in Amsterdam in the early 1990s. The German architects Hans Kollhoff and Christian Rapp claim that the Amsterdam School was their source of inspiration, because of its scale, its city planning capacities and its rich detailing. By the early 1990s, social housing in Amsterdam had devaluated into cheap and technically poor housing, small-scale and uninspiring. The Piraeus building reintroduced scale in the city and brick as the messenger. The brick used was specially designed for the building. More importantly, however, it also became the advocate of the next step in the emancipation of social housing. The façade and floor plans have been detailed in such a way that it is impossible to determine the positions of social housing units, upmarket rental apartments and privately-owned apartments by the composition of the façade. This building has become so influential over the years that last summer, almost 25 years after its completion, ten architects published a book about why this building has been so important for the development of the city and their own work.[1] This project underlines the power of façades in accomplishing political ambitions.

At the moment, some 25 years later, social housing in the Netherlands has hit heavy weather again. Budget cuts by the state, as well as a redefinition of the tasks of housing associations (after serious mismanagement in the 2000s) have rendered them capable of little more than constructing low-cost new housing and renovating existing property. Which is why, from a Dutch point of view, 'Crafting the Façade' was specifically effective in reminding us of the power of tectonics, especially when paired to social ambitions. Even back in the early 20th century there was a lot of criticism of the high cost of Amsterdam School buildings and on the impact of the innovation, which did not go beyond the façade. Behind all the lush brickwork, workers lived in old-fashioned floor plans, all alike, and still far away from what modernism would bring to both interiors and exteriors a few years later. Yet the power of the message, illustrated in abundance in brick, paved the way for further innovations.

1 Hans van der Heijden et al, *Post-Piraeus*, 2017.

The Façade as a Face

nge Beckel

A building façade is our third skin. The first is our dermis, the second our clothes. When we are indoors, our third skin is the building shell—with its façade a face. The face is what we use to communicate with the world outside the building. Façades 'speak' to people in a typologically coded 'building language'. In that sense, façades can express moods and atmospheres. They can radiate a sense of warmth or oppressiveness. Of course, the codes and meanings of a façade's expression vary depending on climate, culture and the traditions of a region. Moreover, the way people read, understand and interpret façades changes not only over time but also from one region to another.

Stacked versus cast

Traditionally, a work of architecture is composed of horizontally arranged blocks of stone cut to size or stacked materials such as brick, and timber floors combined with mortar or another filling material. Such structures are normally supported by massive foundations.

During the period of industrialization, materials for stacking, cladding or cutting to size were replaced by cast substances such as concrete and steel and by large-format glass. The introduction of these materials in the building industry changed our understanding of constructions. From that point onwards, constructions were not only seen as rising layer by layer from the ground. Stacking materials was no longer necessary. Architecture and the building industry abandoned the logic of rising upwards from the ground. Today's buildings are perceived as homogenous bodies and consistent volumes, often cast in concrete.

This homogeneity underlines a building's character as a solitary object that is hardly connected to the ground. One reason lies in the nature of the cast object itself, because cast materials can be produced at a large size, as large as formwork allows. Furthermore, cast objects can be produced anywhere and transported to the designated site. But in contrast to traditional techniques of layering or stacking, the joints in cast objects are hardly visible.

Detached versus bound

The Swiss art and architecture historian and critic Adolf Max Vogt (1920–2013) once distinguished between thoughts, habits and man-made work that are perceived as part of current time, and those understood as standing out of time.[1] The latter become absolute, because those thoughts, habits and pieces of work are universal and hence always valuable.

To come back to the façade as a means of communication, it is obviously more difficult to engage in a close dialogue if the façade is conceived as a universal piece of art. The layers of a building constructed by stacking materials refer in one way or another to human

1 Vogt, Adolf Max: 'Entwurf zu einer Architekturgeschichte 1940–1980', in: ders./Jehle-Schulte Strathaus, Ulrike/Reichlin, Bruno: *Architektur 1940–1980.* Frankfurt a. M./Wien/Berlin, 1980

proportions—insofar as a person can read the proportions or scale of a building. If someone is walking past a clearly proportioned building, they can relate their size to the base, the ground floor or even the first floor. In the case of a building composed of cast materials, it is more difficult to understand the position of floors, especially in the case of a façade with few or no windows.

Identity

As a means of communication, building façades also contribute to a place's identity. And in certain regions, the landscape constitutes part of a community's identity. For people in mountainous regions, topography helps shape identity, notably in a geographical or spatial sense.

Regarding a person's everyday environment, one can speak of a 'native homeland', a place known well. Every person in every town or village on earth is located at a very specific point on the earth's surface. And this point is unique in the world. Both natural and manmade environments therefore contribute to our identity, no matter where we are. Buildings also help define the atmosphere of a place and thus a person's wellbeing. This phenomenon has recently been explored by American art historian Sarah Williams Goldhaben in her book *Welcome to Your World: How the Built Environment Shapes our Lives* (New York, 2017).

We cannot communicate all day. In that regard, abstract façades convey quietness in some way. At the same time, we are part of different communities, and are always interacting with them in some capacity or another. Façades composed of materials that are stacked or cut to size are better communicators in terms of locating ourselves. Façades that are designed, built or crafted in a specific manner pose stronger identities than more abstract ones. We need both, quietness and connectedness. We need a balance of both. We need detached buildings and connected ones; we need abstraction and reification. In the final analysis, life is tangible, corporeal.

The Pain of Separation

Marko Sauer

The façade is in crisis. Even though architects are searching for exits from historical quotation and the dullness of insulation technology, success nevertheless remains elusive. The separating of support, insulation and protective functions should be offering new freedoms—but the profession is still finding it difficult to take advantage.

Houses were largely erected into the 19th century as they had been for thousands of years. Bricklayers and master builders constructed walls from bricks, mortar and stone, carpenters fitted beams and planks. Façades followed similarly long cycles, whereby generations of constructors developed a common expressive language for buildings over the centuries. Simpler buildings took on the qualities of the materials they were built from, expressing their construction through crafted ornaments. The language of more sophisticated buildings played with the possibilities resulting from the working of plaster or the sublimation of the materials, but still remained recognizably rooted in the handcrafted. Even if such materials as steel and in particular reinforced concrete expanded the repertoire of expression, it remained stable over centuries—vernacular architecture is not one of great leaps.

This old relationship between construction and expression began to shift with the arrival of modernism. In Chicago, during the late 19th century, Adler & Sullivan adopted the trend of separating technology and culture, which had its beginnings in the railways. The station concourse itself was bound to the technical side and was wholly subordinated to efficiency, whilst its façade continued to express affiliations with the city. Adler & Sullivan assumed such a strategy for their administrative buildings, juxtaposing modern floor plans with historical façades.

Classical modernism went even a step further, the *plan libre* being one of its foundations, bringing not only unimagined freedoms to the functional context, but liberating architects in the design of façades. The International Style spread these ideas around the globe. What followed was a movement which at its peak promised a revolution, but whose mannerisms ossified into formalism and monotony. The reaction was a critical regionalism, post-modernism and countless regional developments such as Brutalism in Great Britain, Analogue Architecture in Switzerland or, most recently, the handcrafted vernacularism of Bijoy Jain in India. In addition there was also an evasive shift towards more abstraction, which has led in these latitudes to the famous 'Swiss Box'. A glance at the world of corporate architecture suggests that such trends continue, the firms' lustre being reflected smoothly and undisturbed in as much glass as possible.

As much as the examples in this episodic view of the past century differ, they also display a similarity, a separation of space and expression. The intimate relationship between the floor plan and façade dissolved during the 20th century. This cultural separation also manifests itself at the level of construction. During the 1960s, a decisive technical change took place in building: the separating of the tasks of support, insulation and protection. A continuous layer of insulation enabled an actual cultural separation to occur, and the façade to detach from the rest of the building. Where there used to be a cultural and structural link between structure and expression—generally termed tectonics—there is now a lack of interrelations, and perplexity reigns, a perplexity in particular as to how the architect should address this new freedom.

What has been the response to this change? The majority of building production follows the logic of economics and production technology. Plastered external insulation enables any level of environmental sustainability to be achieved, whilst also formally referring to classical modernism, blatantly reduced and obviously misunderstood. Polystyrene envelopes provide pragmatic answers to current challenges. But do they lend the façades an adequate expression of our epoch? Even wooden buildings, where such questions do not possess the same urgency, remain indecisive, seeking expression in reduction. Architects attempt to construct the protective layer of wood as abstractly and with as few joints as possible. Here, too, the result appears emphatically sober compared to historical buildings—even though in the region between Vorarlberg, southern Germany and eastern Switzerland, remarkable contributions have been developed by architectural firms working in collaboration with companies in the wood construction industry.

With regard to cladded façades, the current state of affairs can be studied along Zürich's Europaallee, where aficionados of well-manicured façade design may gather to witness a cycling though of all aspects of tectonics, structure and order. Everything appears very well studied and virtuoso—but nevertheless a stale feeling remains even for a sympathetic viewer. Is this neo-façadism really the cutting edge of developments?

Experiments demonstrating new directions are occurring in somewhat less prominent locations, where approaches to overcoming the separation of tasks appear promising. Three sites may serve as examples: the Bundesverwaltungsgericht (federal court) in St. Gallen employs a façade of supporting concrete columns. In the compact tower, the façade forms an inseparable unit with the pre-stressed roofing panels—it is not a matter of taste as to whether these supports form the façade, but rather a question of structural engineering. The distinctive piers unite groups of two storeys each by supporting recessed intermediate floors at their midpoints. Thus the façade, with its two-storey tiers separated by the projecting visible edges of floor slabs, represents the five divisions of the court. The programme, design and expression of the façade form an inseparable unity. The office building 2226 by Baumschlager Eberle in Lustenau integrates the functions even further, with the mass of the thick brickwork external walls regulating the temperature profile. The height of the spaces, the high windows in their deep jambs and the open floor plans support this effect: the entire building is designed so that the temperature does not fluctuate more than 4 Kelvin, which means that the façade has to also actively contribute. The façade must also make a contribution: the mass of the brick walls balances out the temperature peaks, and the high and narrow windows enable ventilation in the upper part of the space. Thus Baumschlager Eberle again resolves the issues of comfort and efficiency with the means of architecture instead of a massive deployment of technology—as a main characteristic, the façade expresses these virtues with its low percentage of glass and the vertical window proportions. A final example is the Herbal Centre in Laufen, which was created for Ricola by Herzog & de Meuron, together with the earthen building specialist Martin Rauch from Vorarlberg. Here, the façade forms a decisive factor for the use: the thick clay walls regulate the humidity and temperature of the herbal storehouse and are an essential part of the design. Even though the exterior walls are unfortunately not load-bearing here, the example again demonstrates with impressive force what a functionally conceived façade can achieve, and that unique buildings can come about in the collaboration between the planning profession and the building trades. The focus on functionality, expression and production—which is summarized by the phrase "crafting the façade"—bestows on these façades their self-evidence and authority.

Crafting the Façade

rjen Oosterman

The history of modern architecture has been reduced to a simple story: industrialized construction methods applied in large quantities to provide basics for the masses. And, acknowledged, some gems of invention and artistry to spice up the 'stew'. It is a story of embracing technology for the sake of a better future for all, a story of how efficiency and ideology met, producing the slab, the white cube, the skyscraper and more. It is a story of abstraction and reduction, of steel, concrete and glass. The story includes magnificent projects, wonders of engineering and design. But it almost completely excludes the craft side of architecture. In the modern story of progress and an ever-better future ahead, craft is associated with slow, handmade and one of a kind, excluding science and technological advancement. And that is not the story modern architecture wants to present. On the contrary, it presents this opposition between tradition and invention to push its own agenda of happiness for all.

Post-modernism forced cracks in this image and (re)introduced the multitude of expressions that we've had since, including a revaluation of materials and their meaning. Because if one thing was sacrificed on the altar of progress, it was, broadly speaking, specificity and meaning.

There is a second storyline to recall: since Greek and Roman times, architecture has been occupied with being meaningful. As intervention, architecture was and is supposed to express power, to organize and optimize space and program, to add quality on a social level, to give identity to a place. It is supposed to enhance efficiency, to optimize the relation between investment and productivity—the list can be extended. Architecture has always had problems proving it delivered to promise, but most of the time it was simply able to convince through its products—they looked good or performed well, sometimes both at the same time.

But how do you know as an architect how to create a good-looking building? Are there rules? Is there specific knowledge involved? One escape from the dilemma of ambiguity, of the subjective individual preference for one shape over another, of artistic wilfulness, was the claim to truth. As architectural theory had it, architecture represented the God-given order of the universe in all scales and details by creating a coherent system of elements and relations that worked like a language, with words, grammar and style. Good architecture could be differentiated from bad architecture in an (almost) objective way by assessing how well 'the system' had been applied.

To cut a long story short, the truth story was left behind a century or more ago, but the fascination with language, with coherence, and with the interrelation of body and parts stayed. If it wasn't to produce truth, at least it could be expected to produce beauty. Not a bad thing to strive for.

One of the ways to do this, to organize the coming together of materials and construction in a meaningful way, has become known as tectonics. In this theory, architecture is seen as a visual system expressing the building's construction: load-bearing wall, column and beam, balloon frame with cladding, that kind of thing. We're not talking the actual construction alone, but how construction and expression merge into a bigger story: the building should speak of (its) construction.

At this point it becomes crucial how materials meet. That was always important from a practical and aesthetic point of view, but now even more so; to tell a story, one has to be precise. And for this precision a certain knowhow is required, the knowhow of the craftsman, the wisdom of the hand. It is not enough to know your story, to be able to connect to wider themes and topics as architect. You also need to translate these ambitions and ideas to a material level. Again, the level of the craftsman. It may even go further: in a glocalizing world, material itself can be a starting point. To work with local materials on local solutions for issues that may have wider impact.

This is the project and idea that 'Crafting the Façade' is looking into. By looking closely at what colleagues in the past have been doing on a regional level, how they literally made ends meet, we can come to a specific understanding of what architecture can be and how it can be done. Not by copying solutions from Dutch 17th-century brickwork (or Amsterdam Solutions for that matter) in today's projects, or by replicating Swiss-cottage wood connections, taking the past as the source book for today's practice, but by developing a sensibility for detail and for 'making' that can be applied to contemporary materials. That is important for two reasons: firstly, that no architect today can spend a lifetime on becoming an expert in one material (for instance stone)—the speed of design and construction, the variety of assignments and their geographical spread don't allow that kind of localized dedication; and secondly, there is a whole array of present-day materials for which there is no tradition, no craft to draw from.

The larger quest behind this project 'Crafting the Façade' is to ground architecture again, after it went in all these different directions; to reclaim its capacity to be meaningful to the eye and to tell (again) of what it is made.

As 'system of truth', architecture didn't survive, nor as 'system of beauty'. As repertoire for storytelling and as self-referential tectonic system, it is still with us today. But—and this has to be said—even that position of architecture is being challenged today. Not that long ago, architecture claimed to be the mother of all arts, securely seated on top of Mount Olympus. Today it's 'design' that can be considered to be encompassing and all-pervasive. Design (product design, styling, fashion and much more) has no moral or body of knowledge to hold on to. When torn trousers sell twice the price an ordinary pair of jeans make, the notion 'quality' or 'good design' has undergone some fundamental changes.

It is a reality in which an essentially old value system has to find its way. Seen that way, 'Crafting the Façade' is a stubborn attempt to resist 'the flow' and to secure what is considered to be of the essence: the materiality of the story.

Why We Never Talked About Beauty

nne Isopp

When we approach a building, we try to imagine what lies behind the façade. Is it for living, working or learning? The scale, proportion and material of the building and its façade give us a good indication of what is happening inside. The façade is like the business card of a building. You can compare the meaning of a façade for the appearance of a whole building with the features of a human being. It doesn't have to be beautiful in the classical sense of the word, but everything—the materiality, crafting, proportion—has to be coherent to be convincing. The choice of cladding material is not only a question of taste and the expression the architect wants to give the building. It is also a question of functionality, tradition, economy, context (urban or rural) and resources.

In this sense, each region has its own materiality. While wood is a traditional and still common building material in the Alps, you'll find mostly brick façades in the Netherlands, and stone is a traditional material for façades in Scotland. Each community used the material at its disposal. And architects still know how to use these traditional building materials for creating modern architectural forms and expressions.

Different regions, different approaches

When you look at a modern building faced in wood, brick or stone, you may see whether the architect succeeded in designing a façade in the logic of the building, its function and the materiality of the structure. Each material has its own logic and there are different aspects to be considered from the practical and architectural perspectives.

When you look at the work of the Austrian architect Bernardo Bader, you learn a lot about tradition, resources and expression. Bernardo Bader built his own detached house out of wood. He used sixty spruce, elm and fir trees, taken from his wife's wood. The tectonics of the house are a combination of concrete elements for load-bearing parts and an inner and outer wooden shell. The house is clad with wooden shingles, so you do not see what the tectonics of the building are like. That is a traditional way of building with timber, which Bernardo Bader combined with modern fabrication and concrete elements, so that the building is very modern yet tells us a lot about tradition, resources and expression.

To understand the use of a cladding material, you also have to understand how the construction industry works. In this sense it was very interesting to listen to the Dutch architect Hans van der Hejden. He is known for his social housing projects in Amsterdam, where he mostly uses prefabricated façades made of brick. In his work, Van der Heijden is very much concerned with tradition, economy and design. He says that he draws coloured façades right at the start of the project. This way of working shows how the construction industry works in the Netherlands. The architect is not involved in the construction process until the end, so he has no influence on how things are handled in the construction phase. That's why Van der Heijden tries to define as many details as possible beforehand.

Hans van der Heijden also stresses that the choice of material and the way a façade is constructed has to do a lot with financial considerations. You can talk the whole day about honesty and true tectonics, but in the end, you have to work within the financial budget of your client. That's why full bricks are not often used for social housing projects. Instead, thin cladding bricks are attached as a finish.

Scottish architect Neil Gillespie instead uses lots of materials in his work, always determined by the inner logic of the building and its construction material. Although stone is a traditional façade material in Scotland, it seems to be increasingly replaced by glass, brick and other cladding materials. This may be due to the fact that stone is now used as a cladding veneer, in a similar way to the modern use of brick panels.

Why did we never talk about beauty?

At the beginning of May 2017, students, teachers, architects and journalists met at the University of Liechtenstein in Vaduz to talk for a day about the crafting of façades, focusing on the use of stone, brick and wood. We got to know the work of Bernardo Bader, Hans van der Heijden and Neil Gillespie, as well as that of the students. When you start to think about a material, you have to ask yourself: What does it feel like? Is it soft or hard? Is it easy or difficult to craft? Do you use it in big or small units? Can you build something out of the material with your own hands in order to experience the properties of the material? These questions are important when it comes to teaching methods. Students approach stone, brick and wood in different ways.

From that perspective, wood and stone are total opposites, and brick is somewhere in-between. Stone is the hardest of the three materials. It is heavy and difficult to craft. In Scotland stone is a traditional building material, so the workshop on stone was held in Glasgow. A student who attended this workshop told us that, in contrast to the workshops on wood and brick, they could not work with the material on their own because it was too dangerous. Learning about stone was all done visually: by looking at ancient buildings and drawing 1:10 sections, while the session on wood in Vaduz was combined with a 1:1 workshop. The students really appreciated the opportunity to build something with their hands. Wood is a very rewarding material because it offers an opportunity to build something on your own.

After leaving Vaduz via Vienna, I realized that we talked for a whole day about the many aspects of crafting façades, but we never used the word beauty—although the projects we saw during the lectures were beautiful: the detached house by Bernardo Bader, the gallery in Liverpool by Hans van der Heijden (the white brick walls inside the gallery, which look so elegant in white, contrasting with the rough surface of the stone), and the Maggie's Centre in Glasgow by Scottish architect Neil Gillespie (with a beautiful gridded fence made of brick). Why did we never talk about beauty? We talked about honesty, tectonics, and a lot of educational experiences. Maybe it was because at university you have to focus on single aspects. Or as one of the teachers said: "We do not teach a style but a tool."

But, in my opinion, it's all about beauty in the end. You feel it when the choice and use of the material on a façade is an exact response to the questions of context, function, resources and expression. So please do not forget this aspect.

3

NINE FAÇADES

Studios

Stone

09.2015–01.2016
Amsterdam,
Glasgow, Vaduz

Brick

02.2016–06.2016
Amsterdam,
Vaduz

Wood

09.2016–01.2017
Amsterdam,
Glasgow, Vaduz

In our design studios all participating students were working on the same studio topic. One of the three project partners was responsible for the content and organization of one design task, which was then carried out jointly. By choosing the materials stone, brick and wood, we placed a clear focus on the building traditions present in the three countries: Brick in Amsterdam, Stone in Glasgow and Wood in the alpine region of Liechtenstein. The sites and also the topics stand for a characteristic task in these three countries. The integrated workshop with the analytic drawings and the hands-on part enriched the studio projects.

Geological Society of Glasgow

The assignment focused on the design of a building for the Geo
logical Society of Glasgow in the city centre. The rocks and scener
around Glasgow make it one of the finest regions in Britain in to gai
an understanding of geology. Founded in 1858, the Geological Soc
ety of Glasgow has enjoyed a proud history of activity and achieve
ments. The chosen site was a plot measuring 15 by 30 metres in th
Glasgow grid. During the whole design process, students adopte
a spatial and tectonic design approach and worked three-dimer
sionally with models, sketches and sections. During the first thre
weeks, each student carried out research on geology and on th
typology of an institute devoted to geology. Everyone compiled
personal catalogue with references, notions, models and drawing
After four weeks, the material merged into a spatial concept for th
institute building. Students then translated the spatial concept int
a design that displayed consistency in its architectural, logistic, ser
sory and tectonic aspects. In the final phase, they refined their design
in relation to the site and the geological history of Glasgow, the spati
programme, and the use of stone.

1 Blended Malt, Max Meijer
2 Versteinert, Milena Fischer
3 Centre for Geology, Rogier van den Brink

Blended Malt

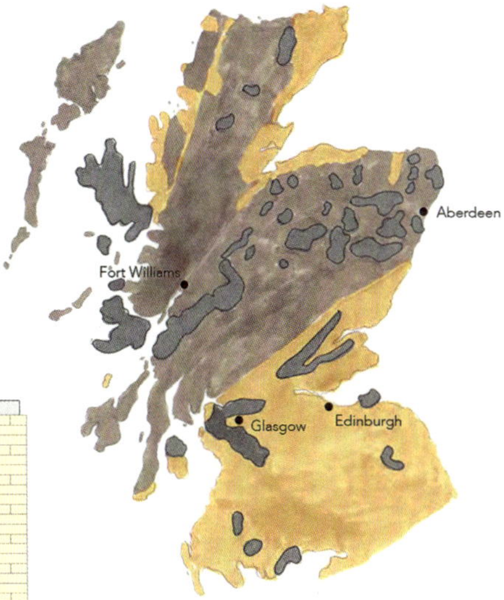

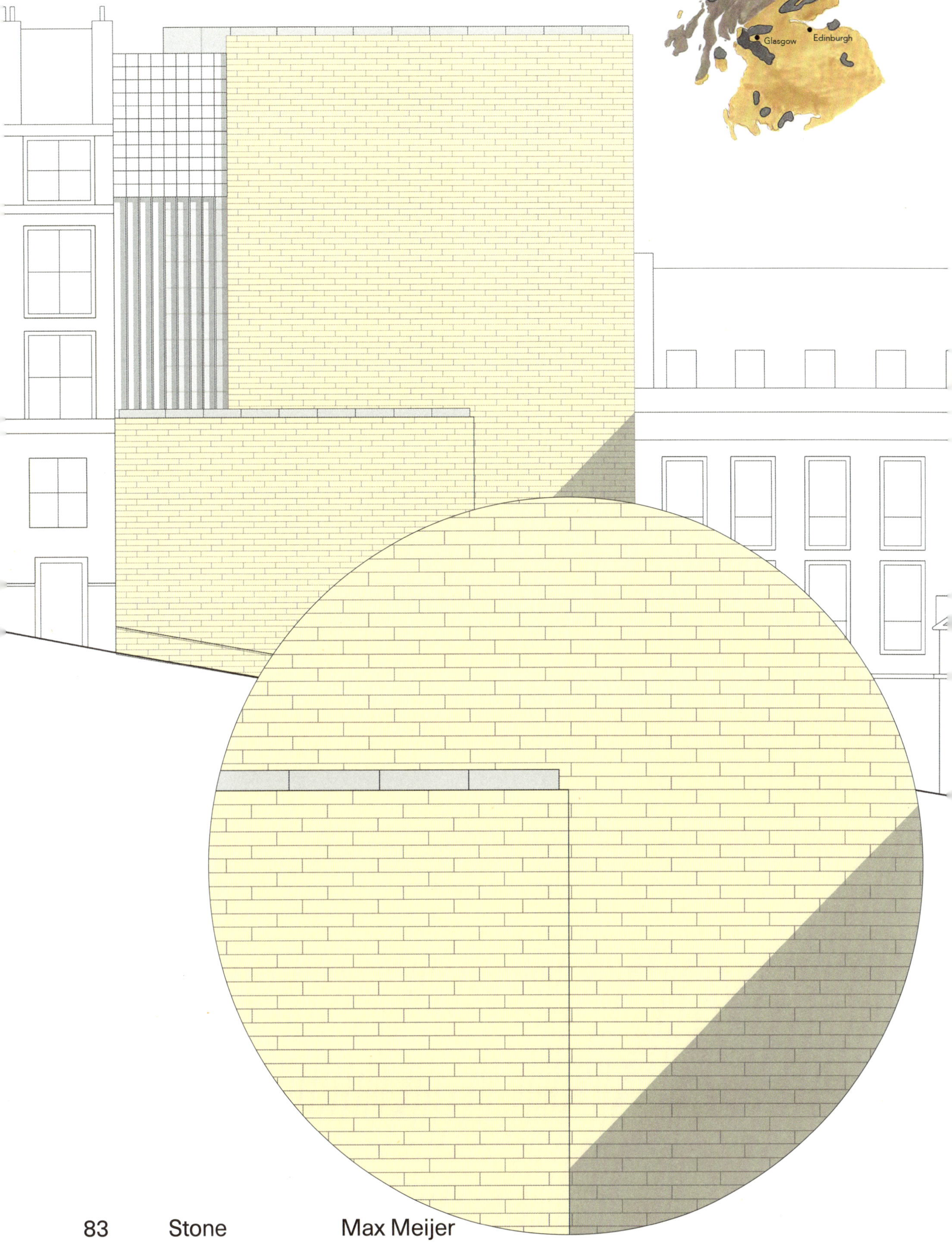

Blended Malt

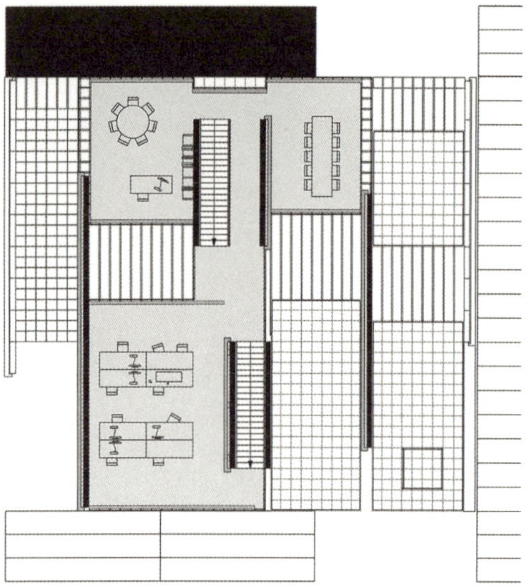

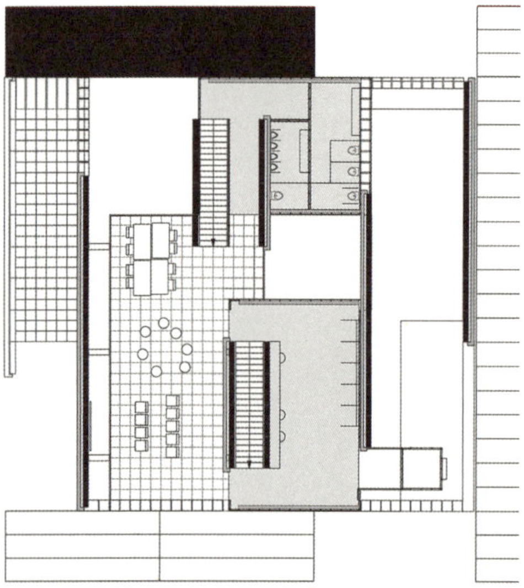

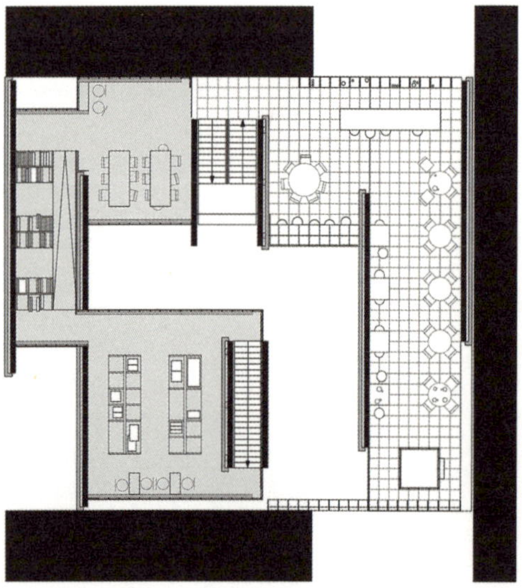

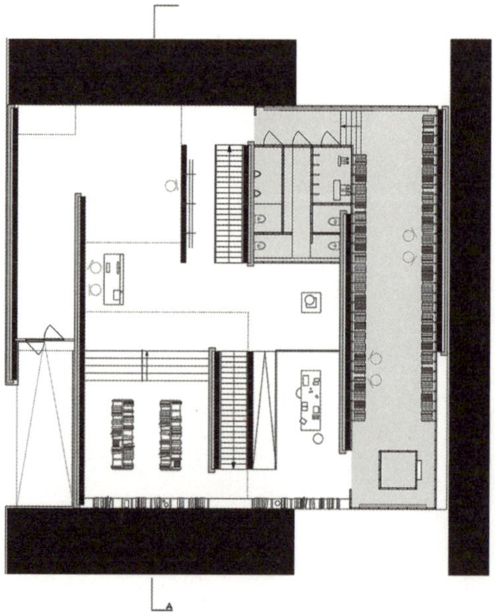

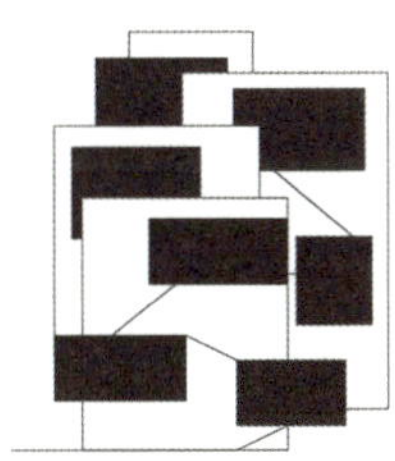

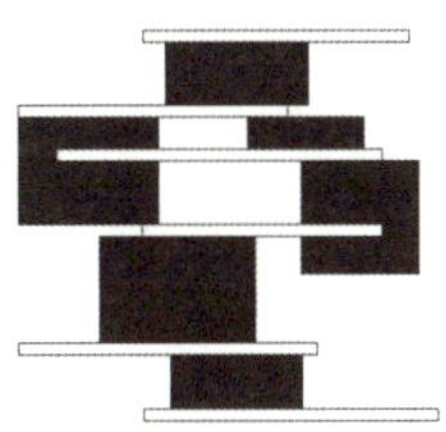

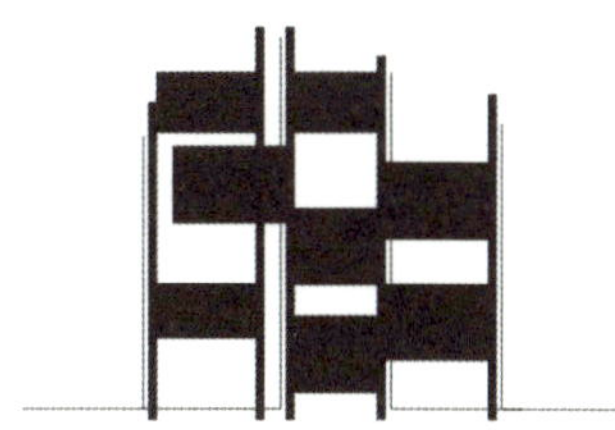

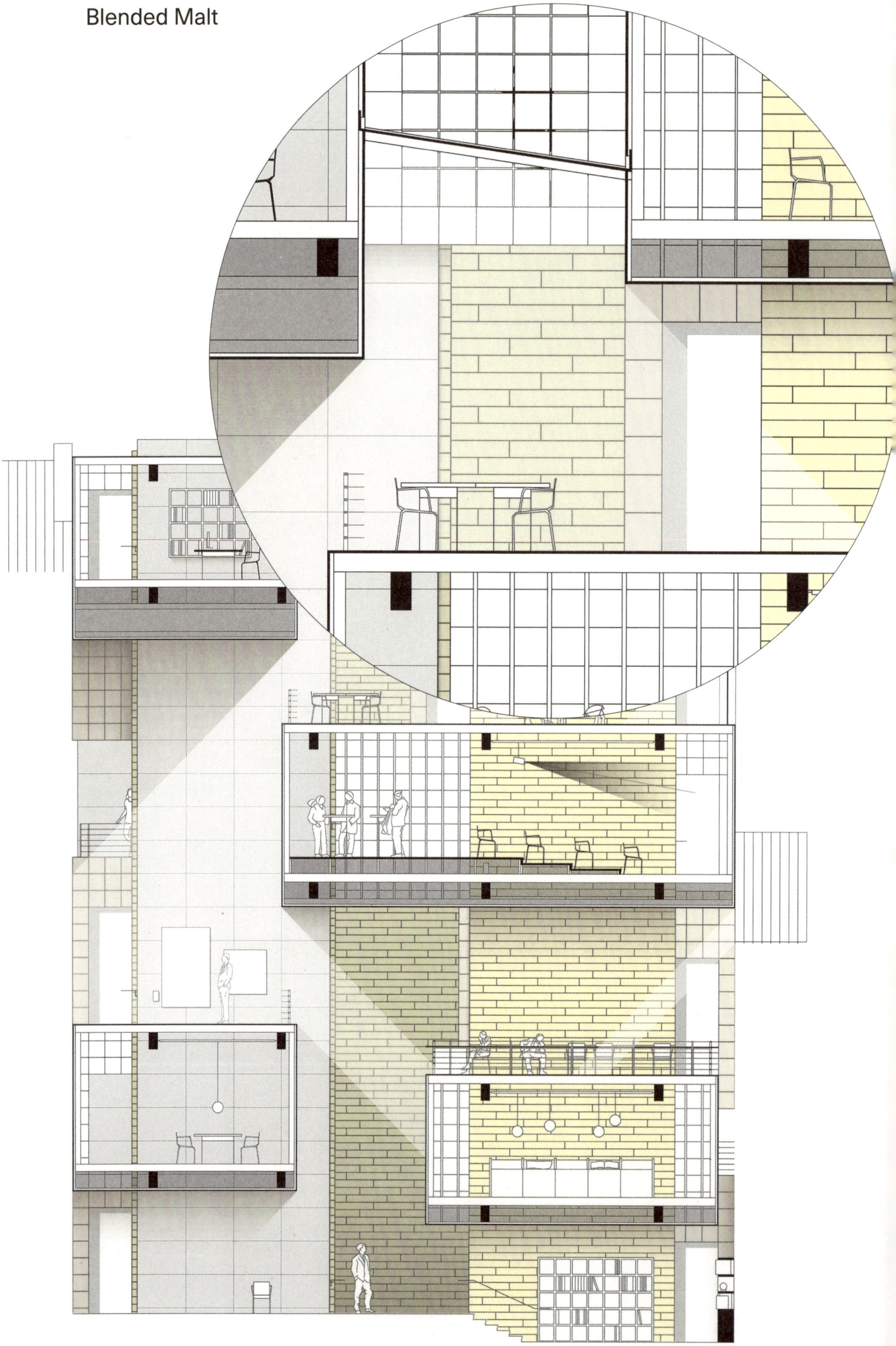

Versteinert

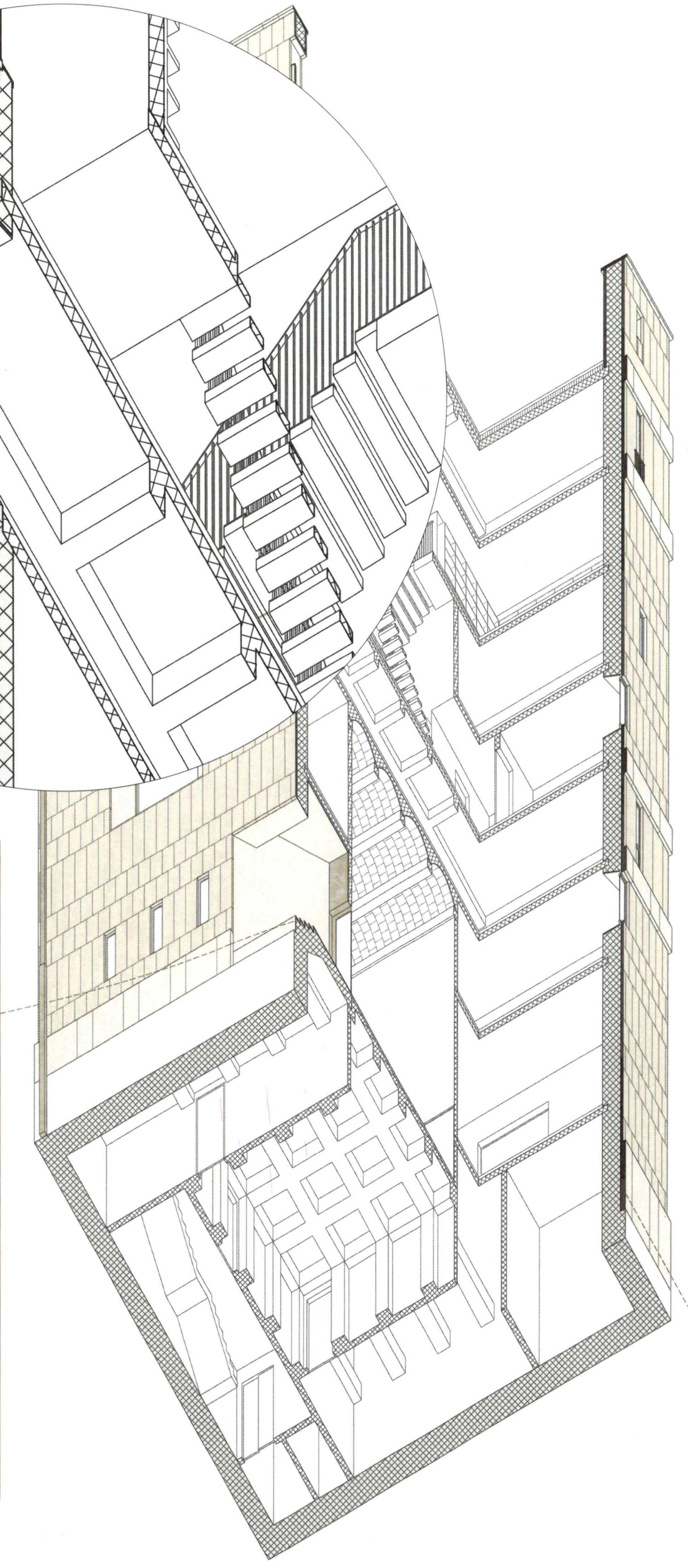

Centre for Geology

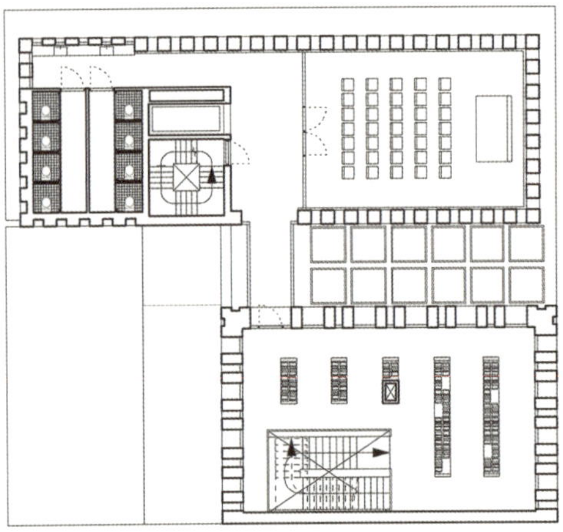

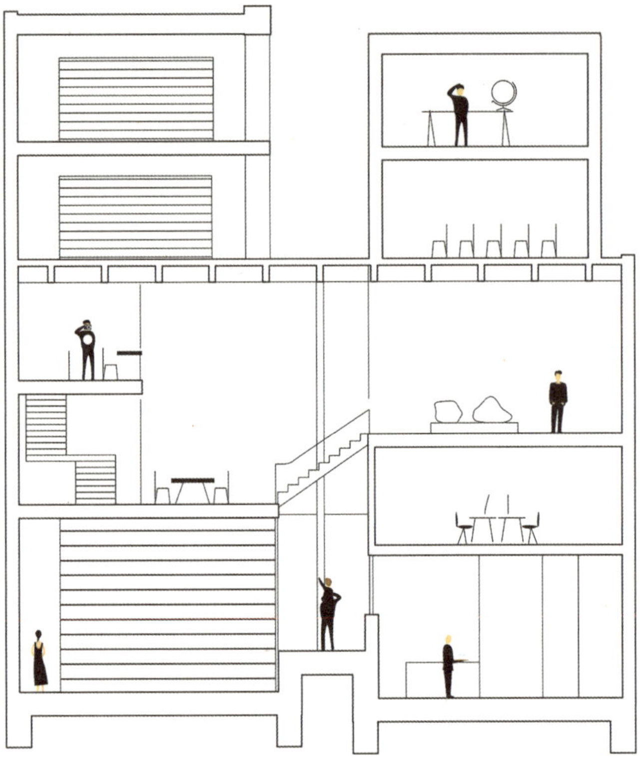

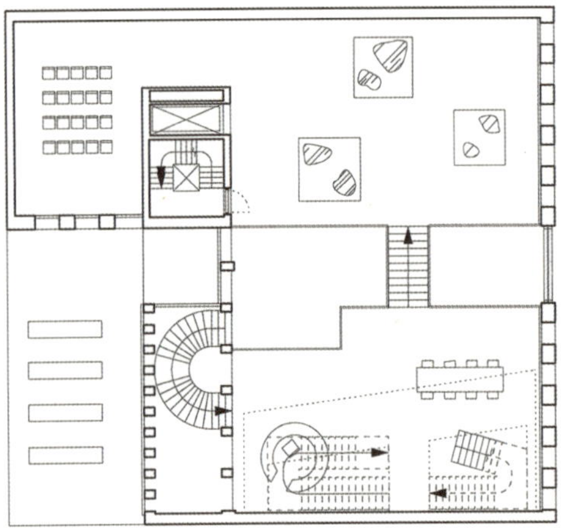

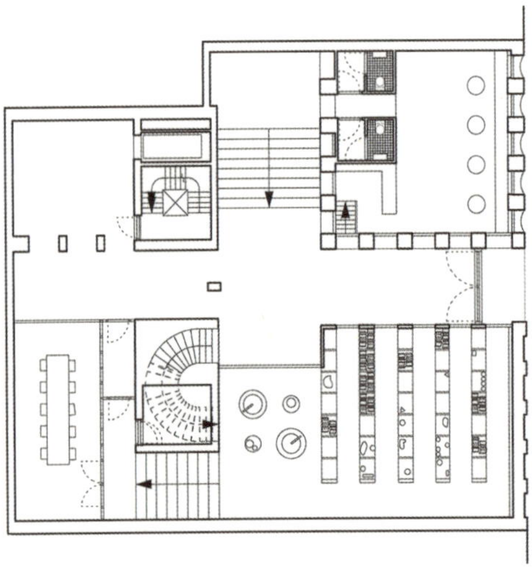

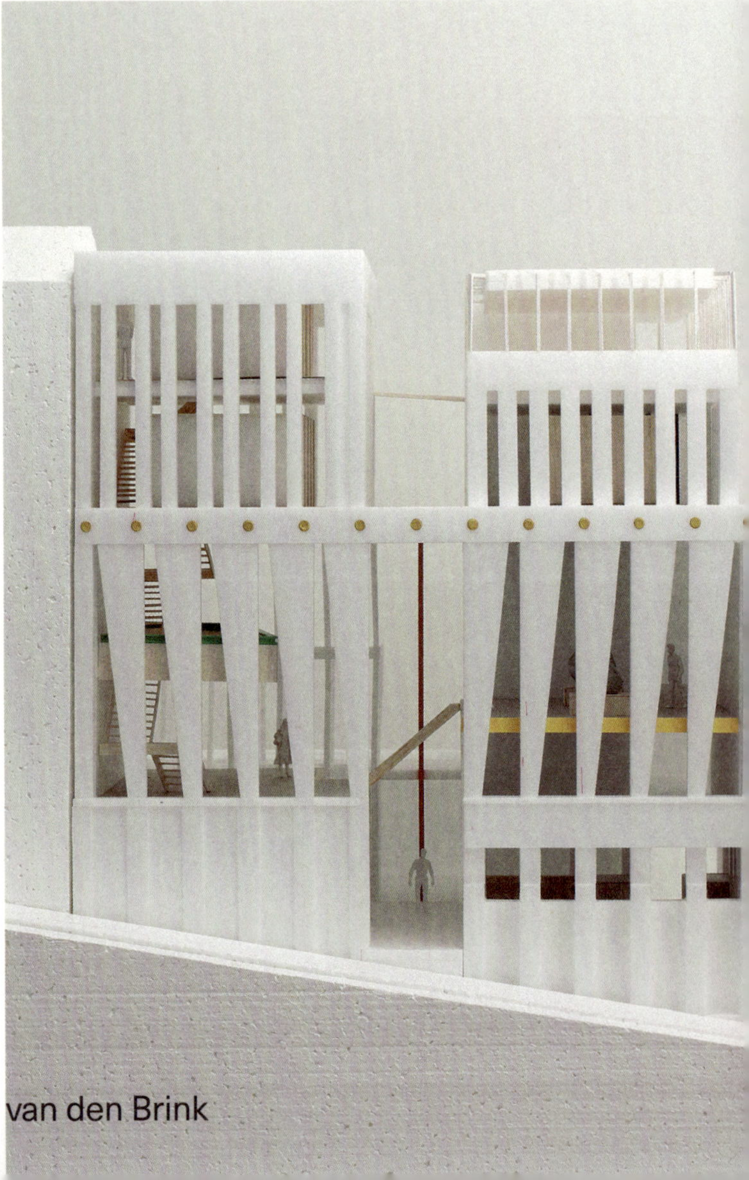

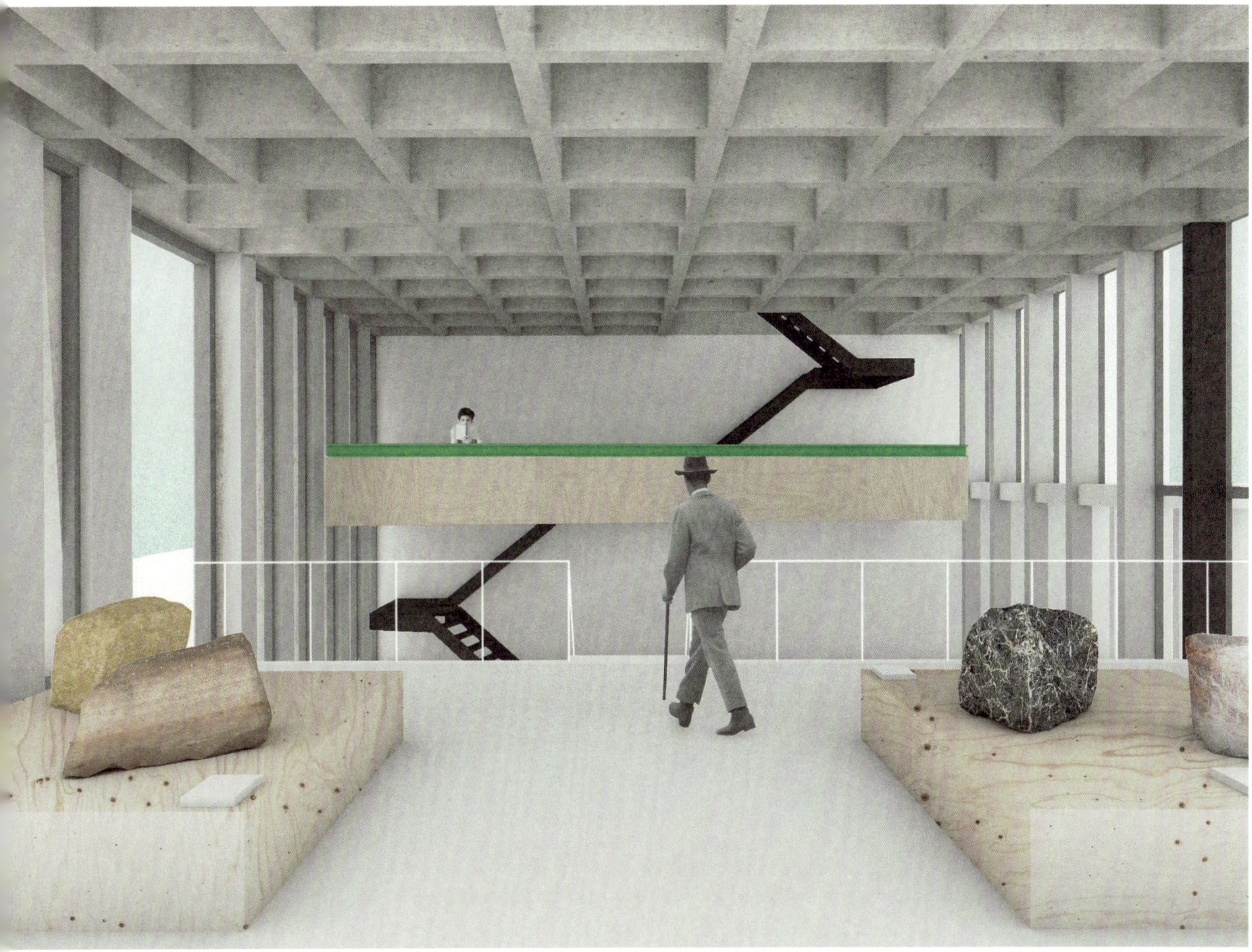

The assignment proposed new accommodation for the Dutch Bric Centre in a former industrial area of Amsterdam North overlookin the River IJ. The multi-tenant building accommodated the Royal Dutc Society of Brick Manufacturers and the new European Ceramic Wor Centre. Students were asked to explore the architectural possibilitie of brick façades that are load-bearing, in contrast to today's conver tional cavity wall constructions. This construction method provide a possible answer to the challenges of ever-increasing insulatio demands. The studio offered an introduction to brick as a materia and to tectonic thinking by means of theoretical reflection, analysi of reference projects, and practical hands-on exercises. Tectonic here was understood as the conscious integration of technique an art, construction and beauty, making and appearance. Students wer invited to relate to one of the tectonic traditions and develop thei own architecture. Neither the material brick nor the requirement o a self-supporting façade formed a limitation. Instead, both seeme to have a liberating effect, offering the freedom of in-depth explora tion and continued focus, while tectonic thinking offered a reflectiv framework. The student work convincingly showed that the materia brick and tectonic thinking can generate a wide variety of desig positions, open to contemporary interpretation. Brick, a material wit a centuries-old tradition, and tectonic thinking proved to be bot relevant and vibrant today.

4 Amsterdam Brickwork, Ewelina Langer
5 Netting Bricks, Viviane Göbel
6 Brick and the City, Jesse Mommers

Amsterdam Brickwork

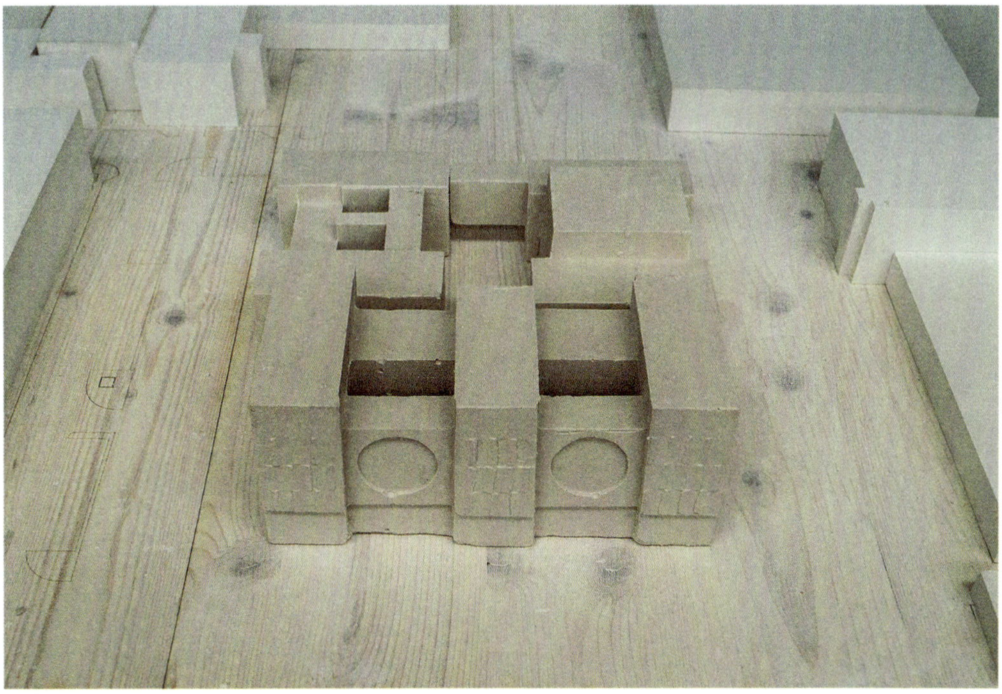

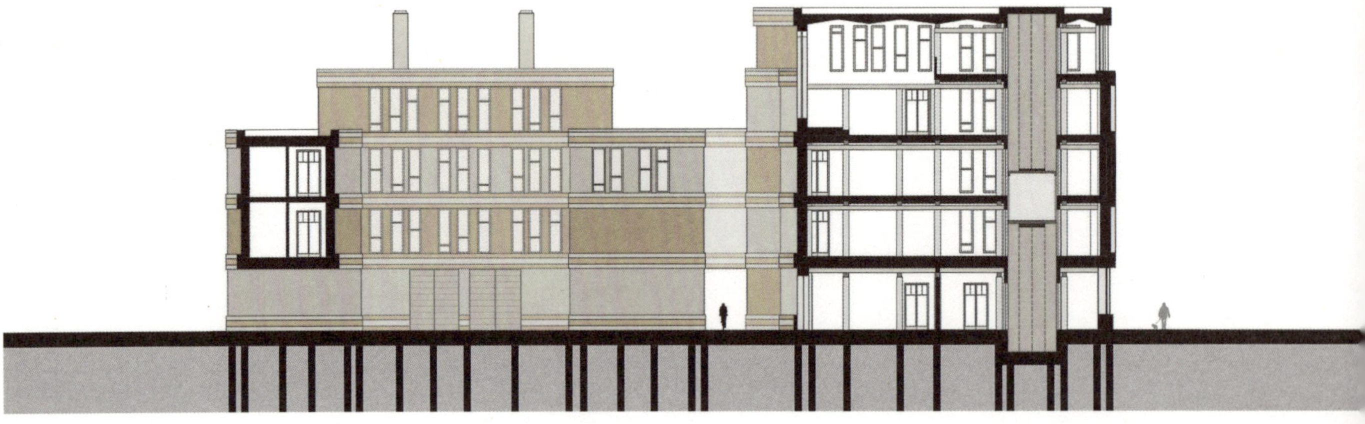

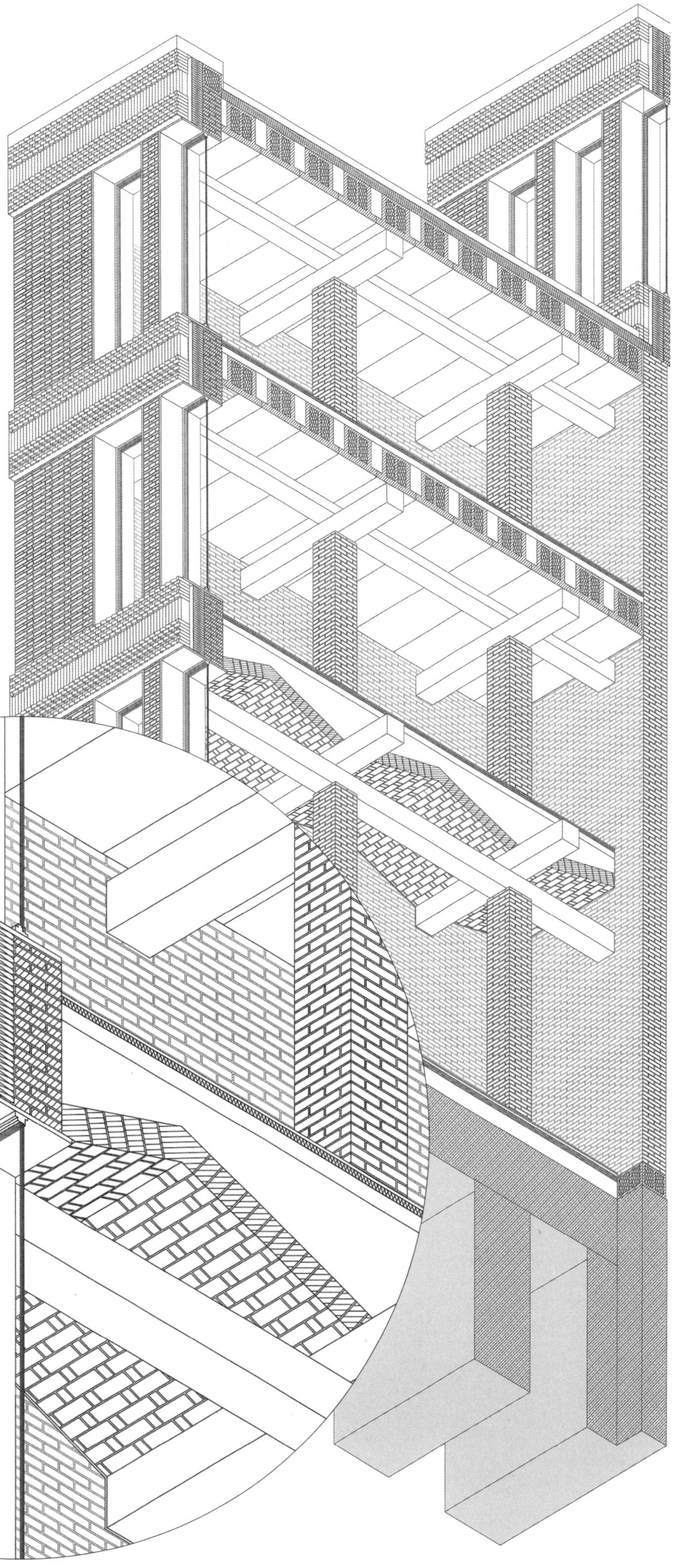

Netting Bricks

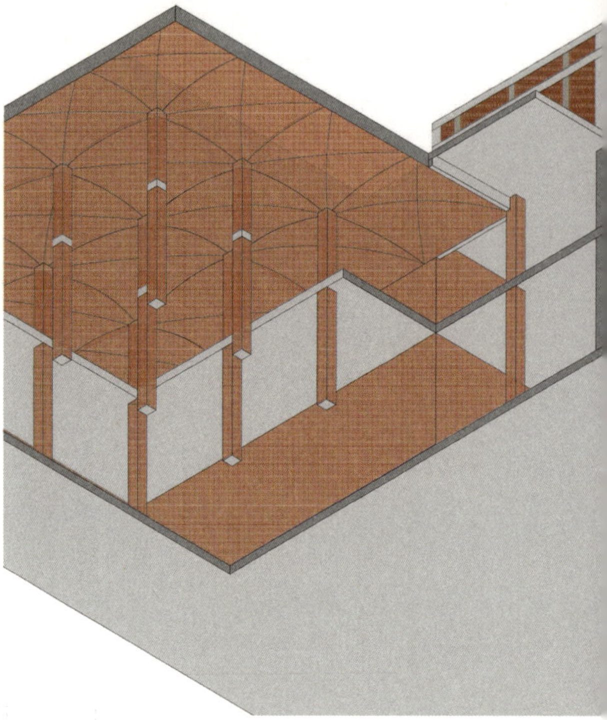

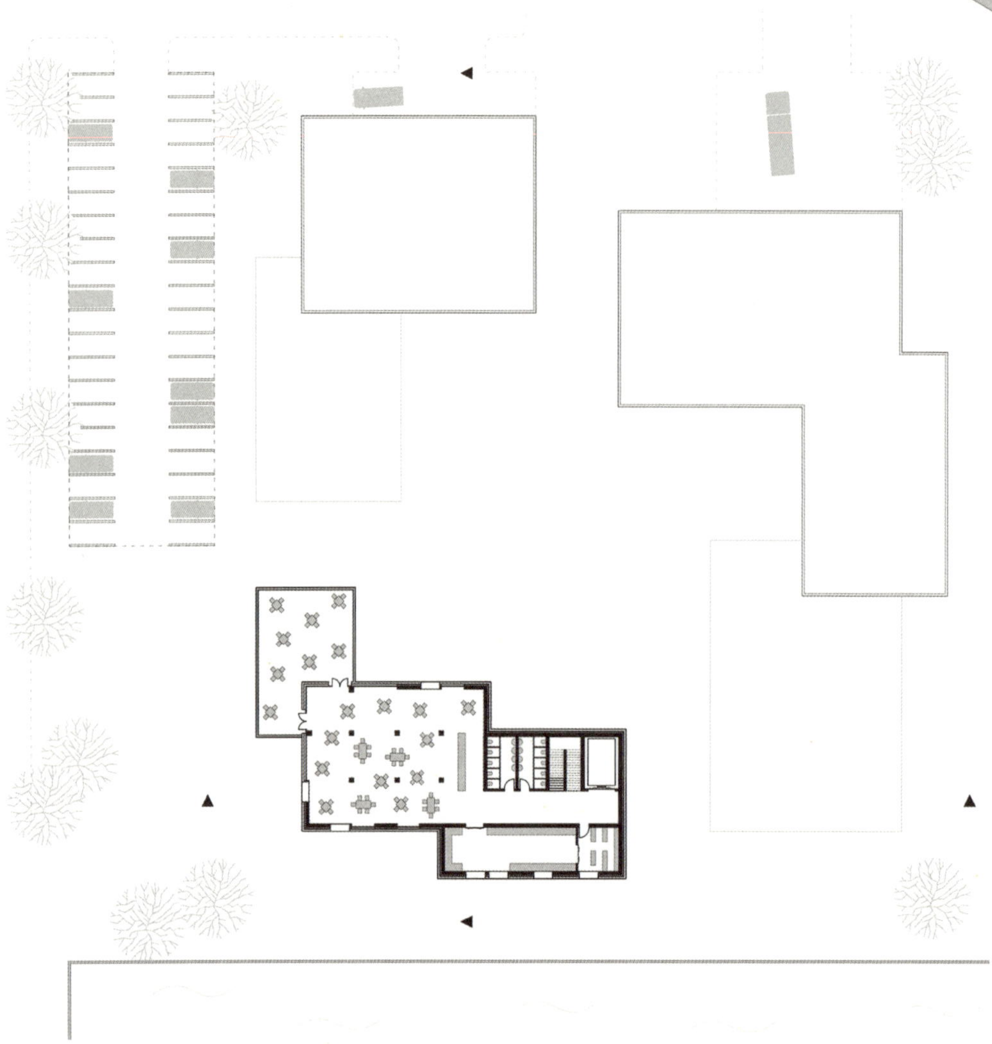

Netting Bricks

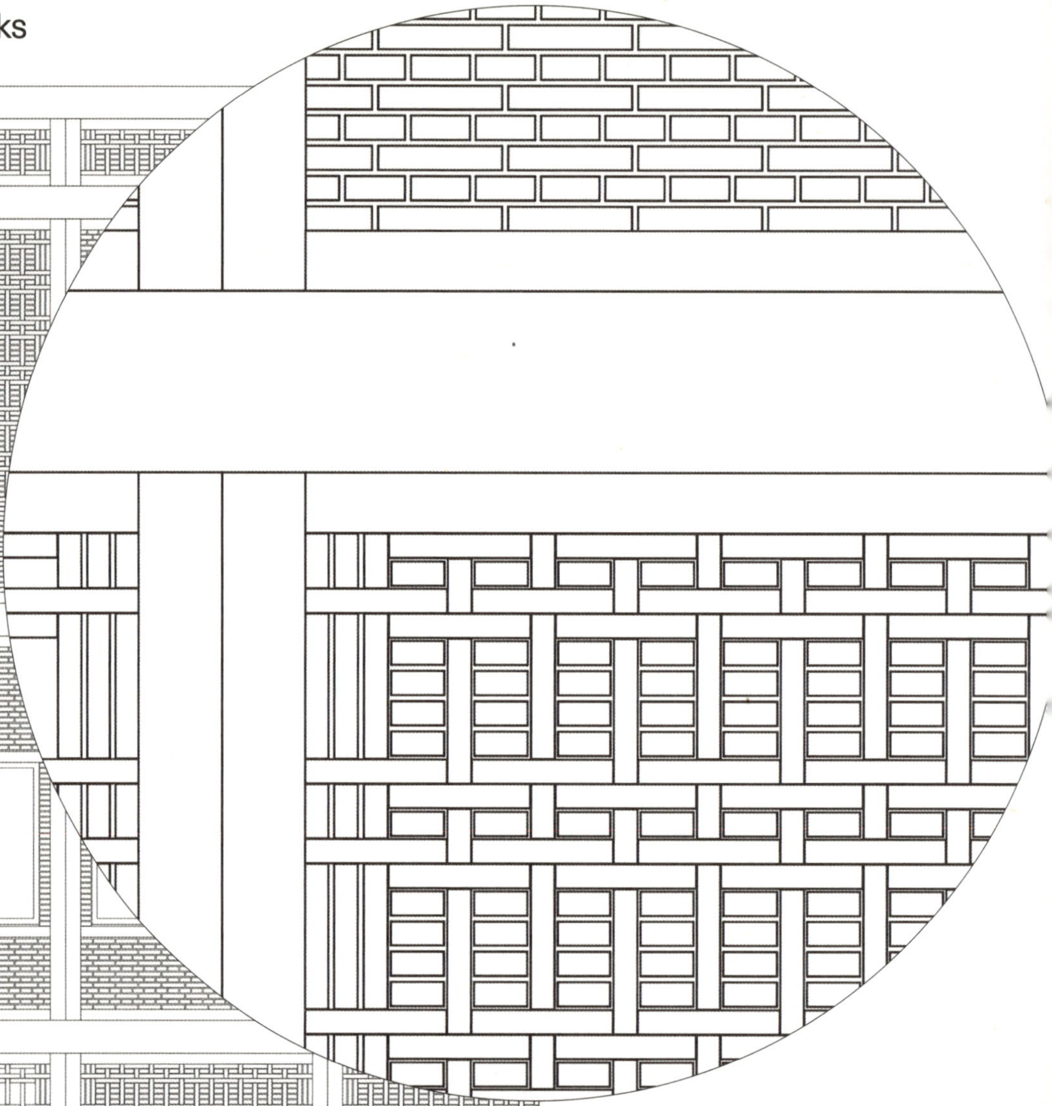

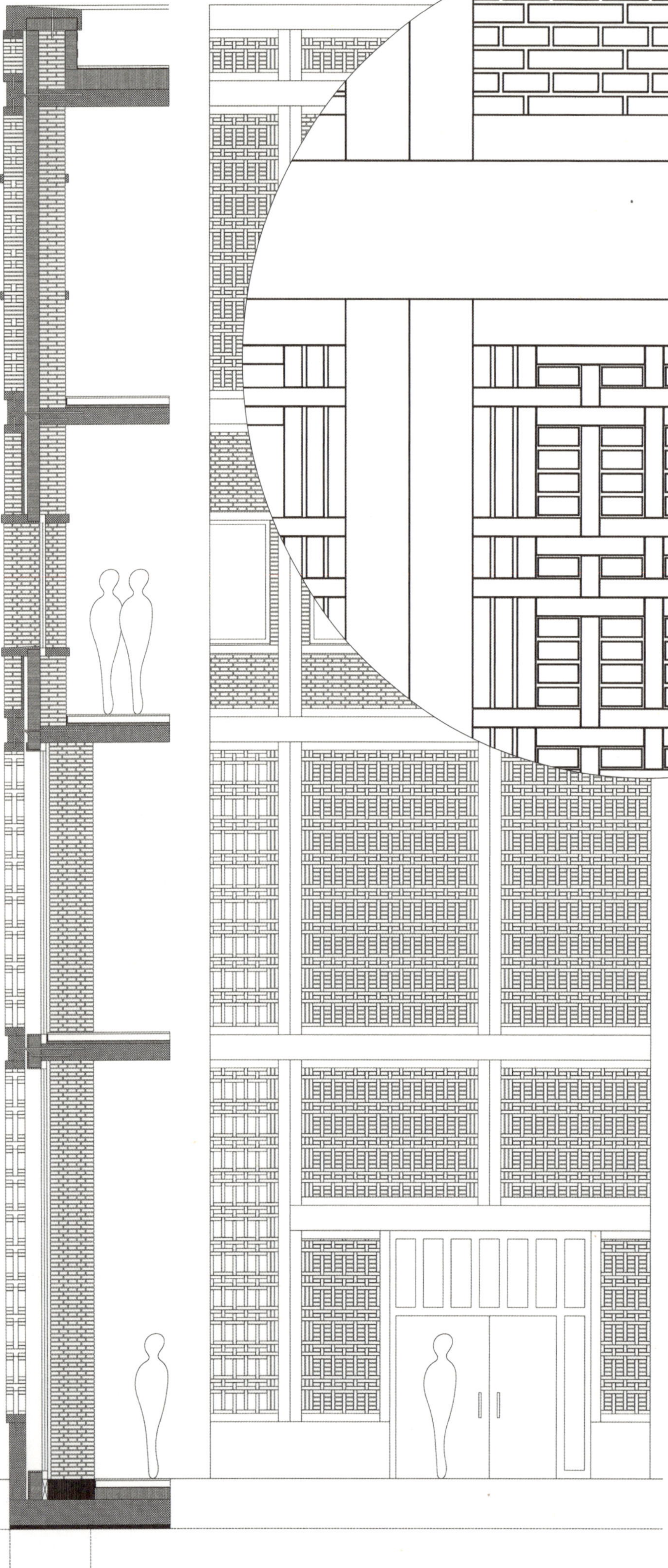

Brick and the City

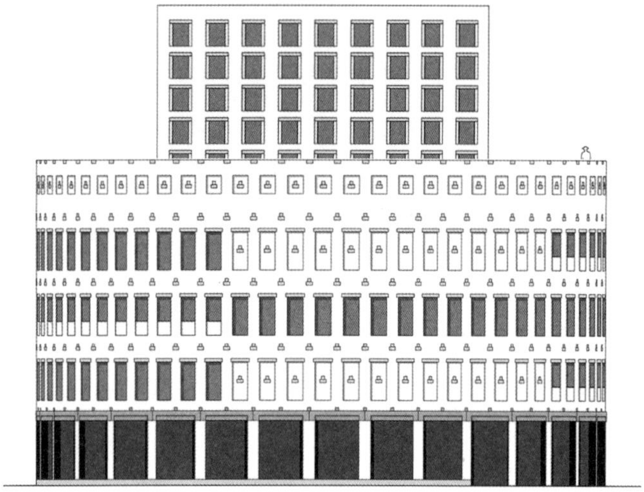

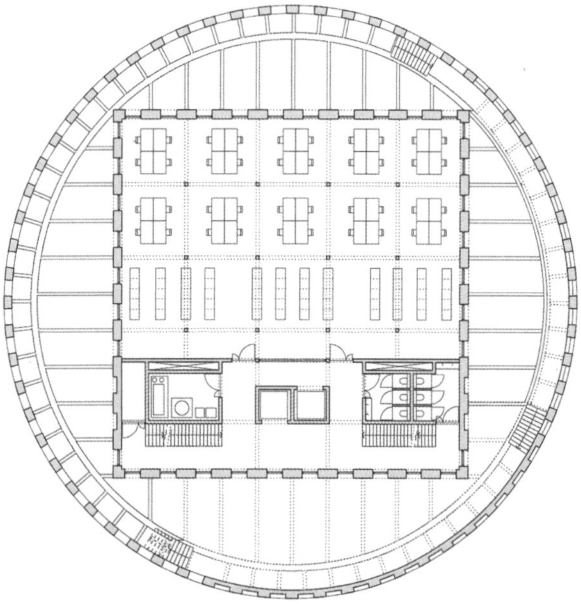

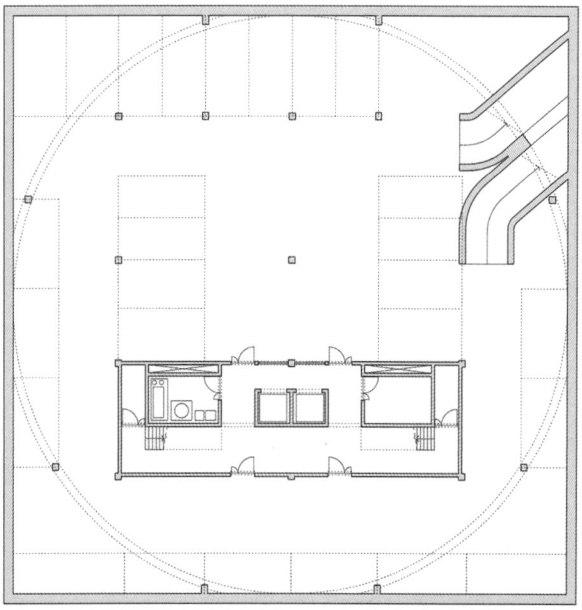

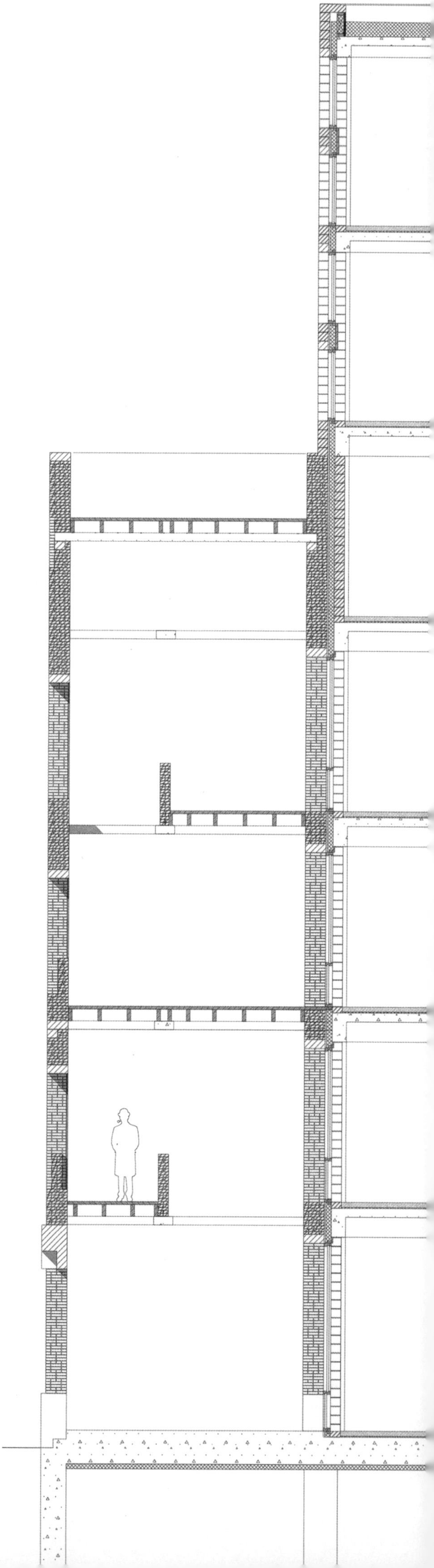

Alpine Lodge

The wood design studio of the 'Crafting the Façade' project focuse on the theme of the façade and was dedicated to timber building and their role as mediators of different cultural identities. The assign ment was to design an inn at an altitude of 1500 metres on a mountai ridge in the Liechtenstein Alps. The Alpine Lodge was set on stee topography in the Rhine valley and had to adapt to the extraordinaril different seasons. Rooms for sleeping and eating were groupe around a core that was developed by each student to accommodat a different function, such as a therapy area or spa. Design approache were influenced by research into historical, contemporary and anon ymous timber architecture in European and Asian building cultures A careful analysis of timber joints that reflect the centuries-old wis dom of carpenters and builders led to the development of new timbe joints that could renew the role of the material in the field betwee structure, construction and tectonic. Students examined the inte action between design and materials to find answers to contemporar requirements. In addition to plans and models, large-scale mock-up and hand-drawn sections and elevations at scale 1:10 conveyed th spatial, structural and material aspects of the designs.

7 Consciousness of Silum, Anne-Lea Pfistner
8 The Wooden Inn, Tristen Vreugdehil
9 Sanctuary, William McRoberts

Consciousness of Silum

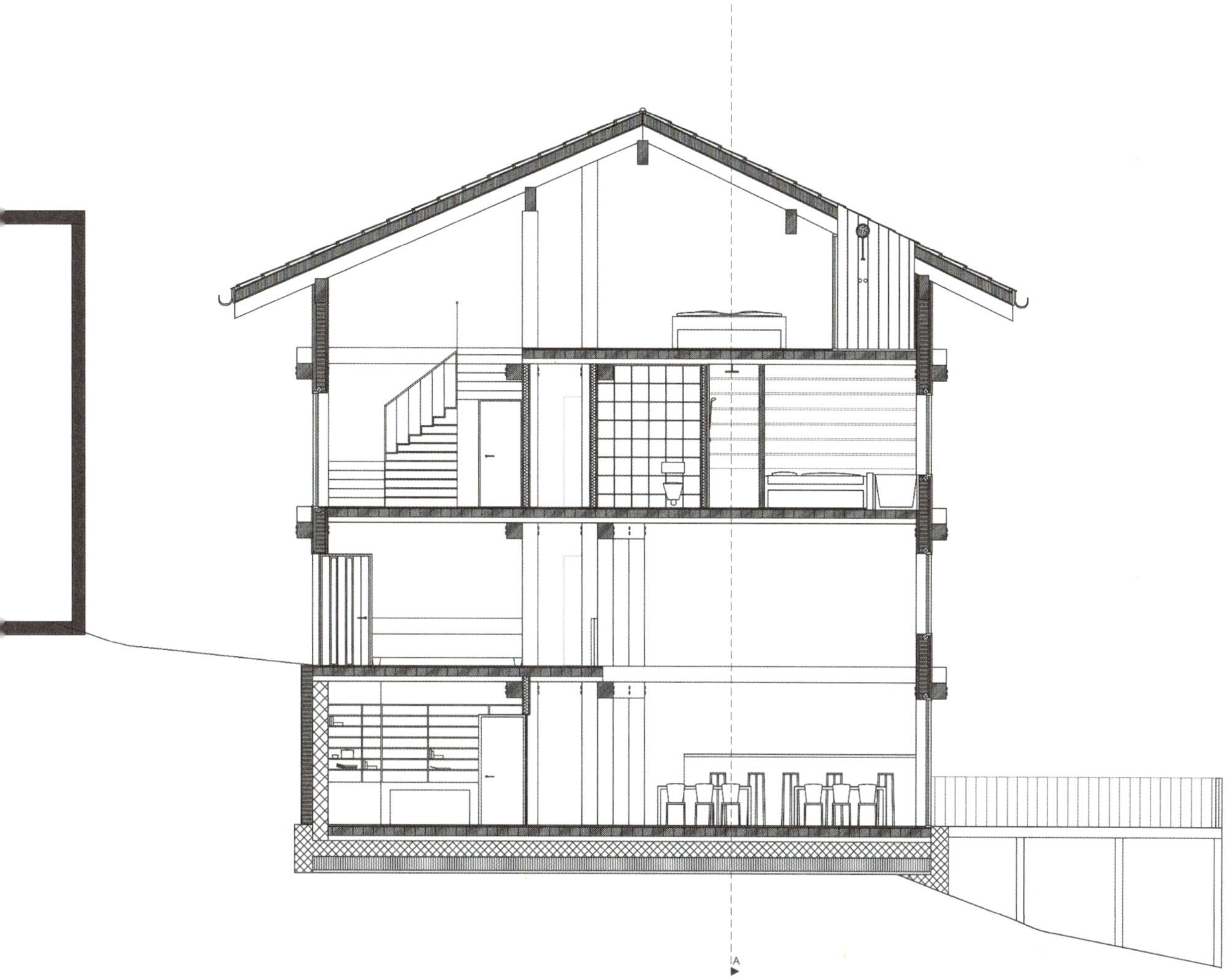

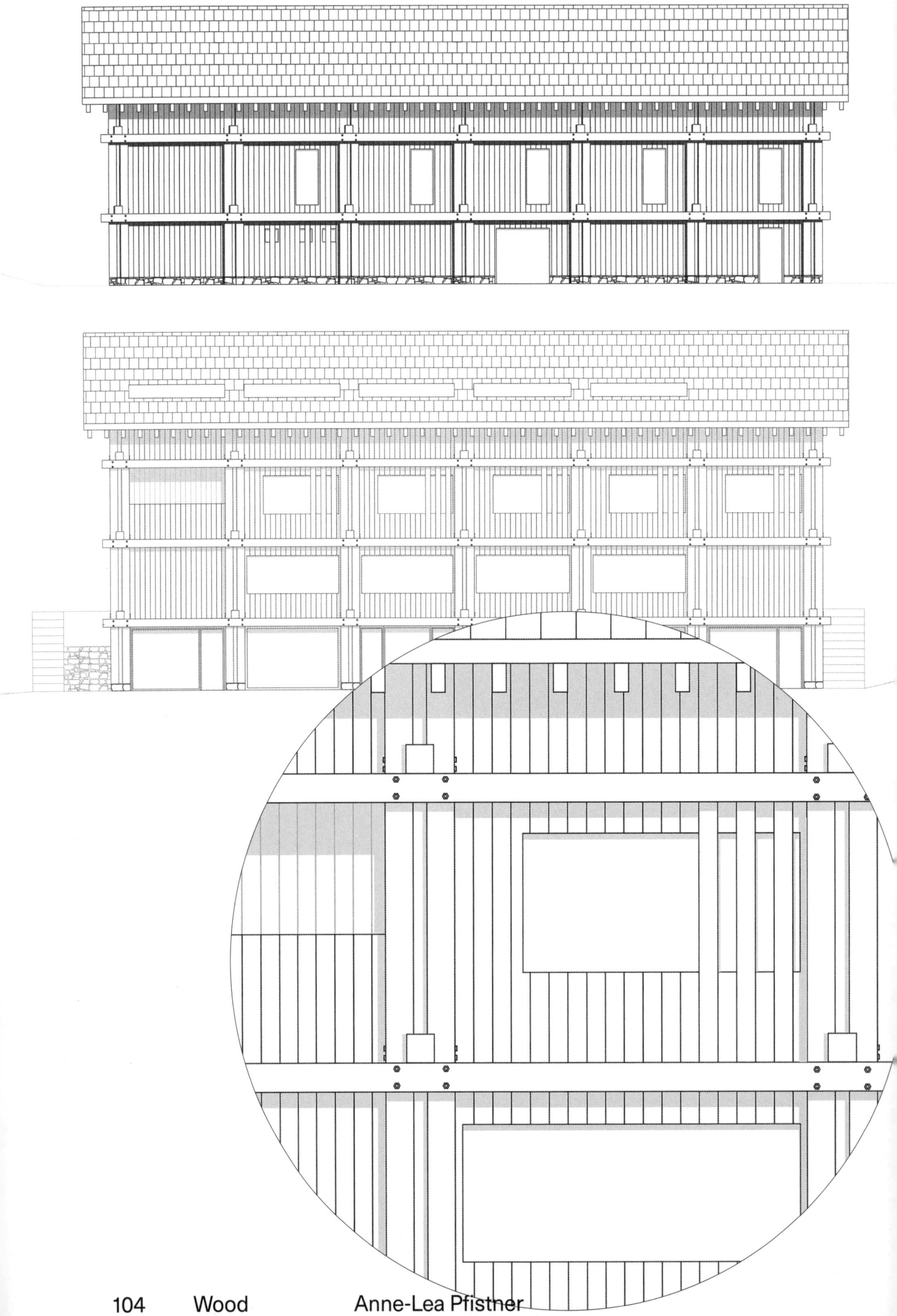

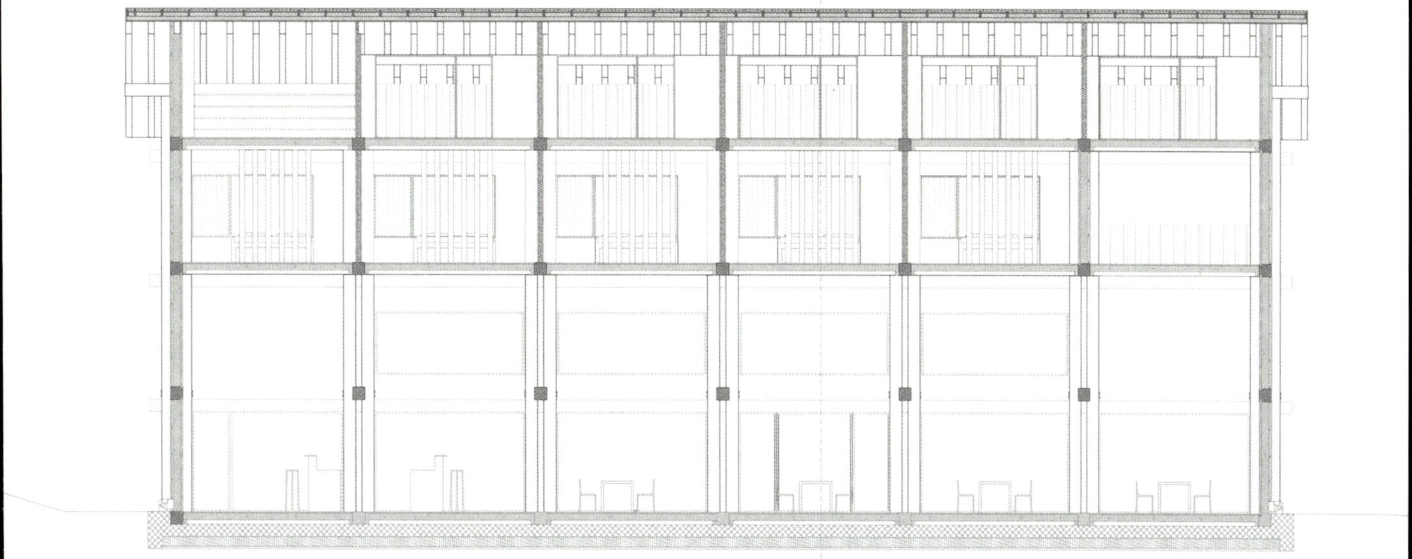

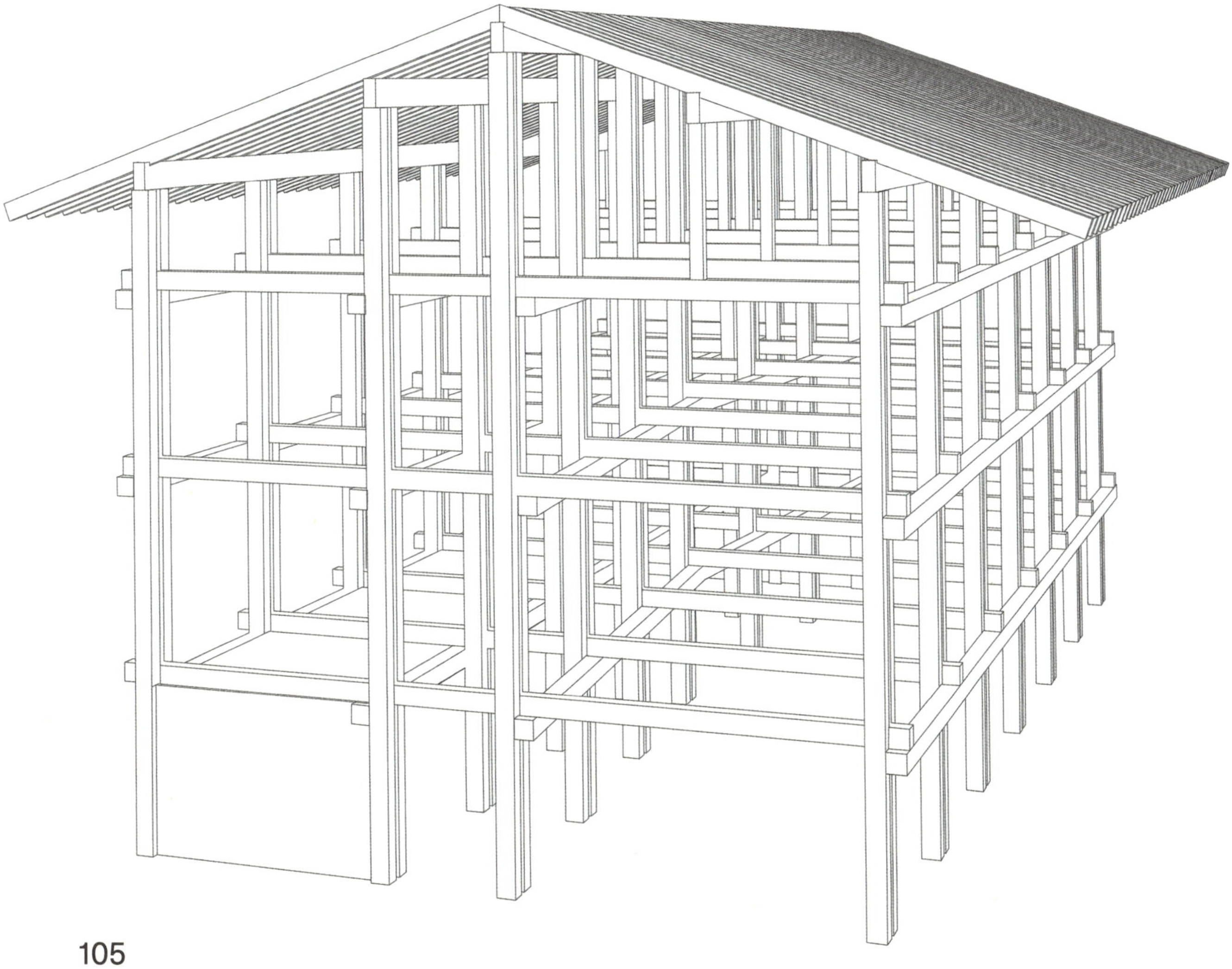

The Wooden Inn

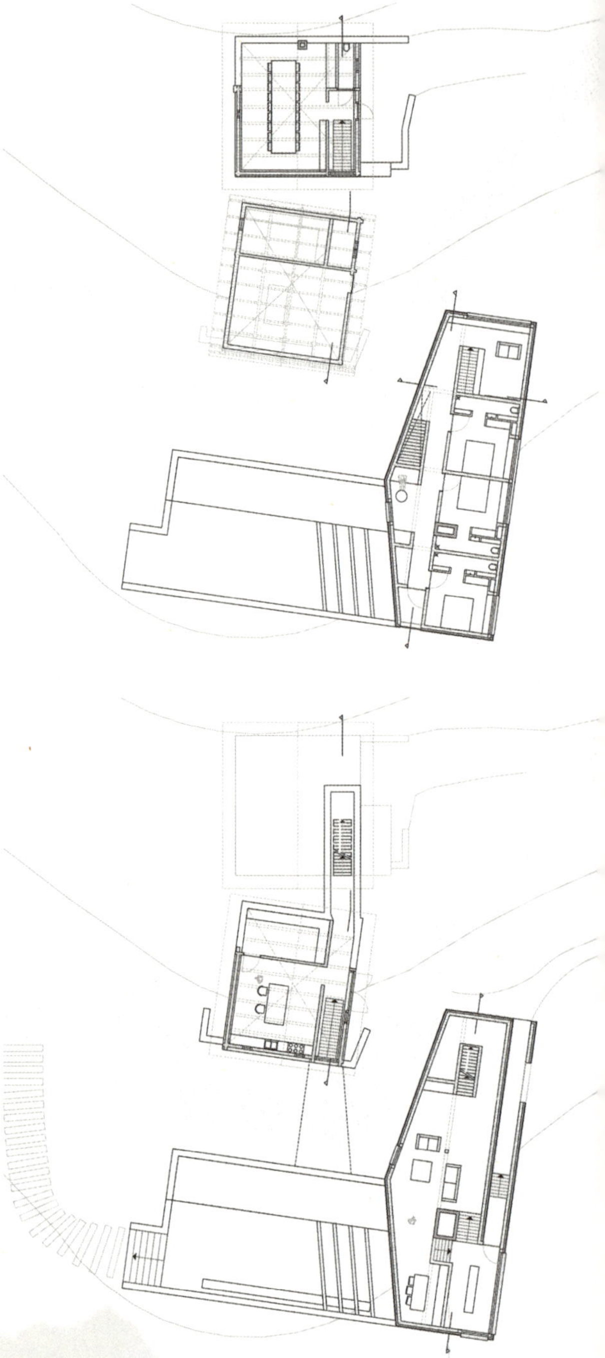

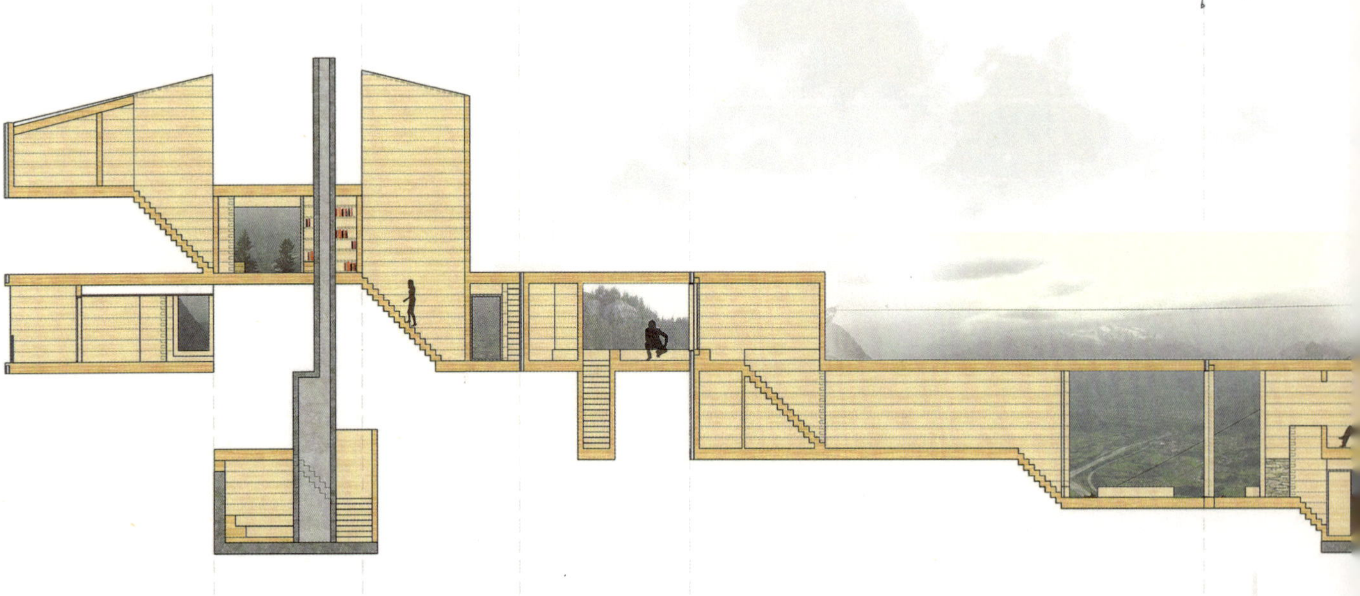

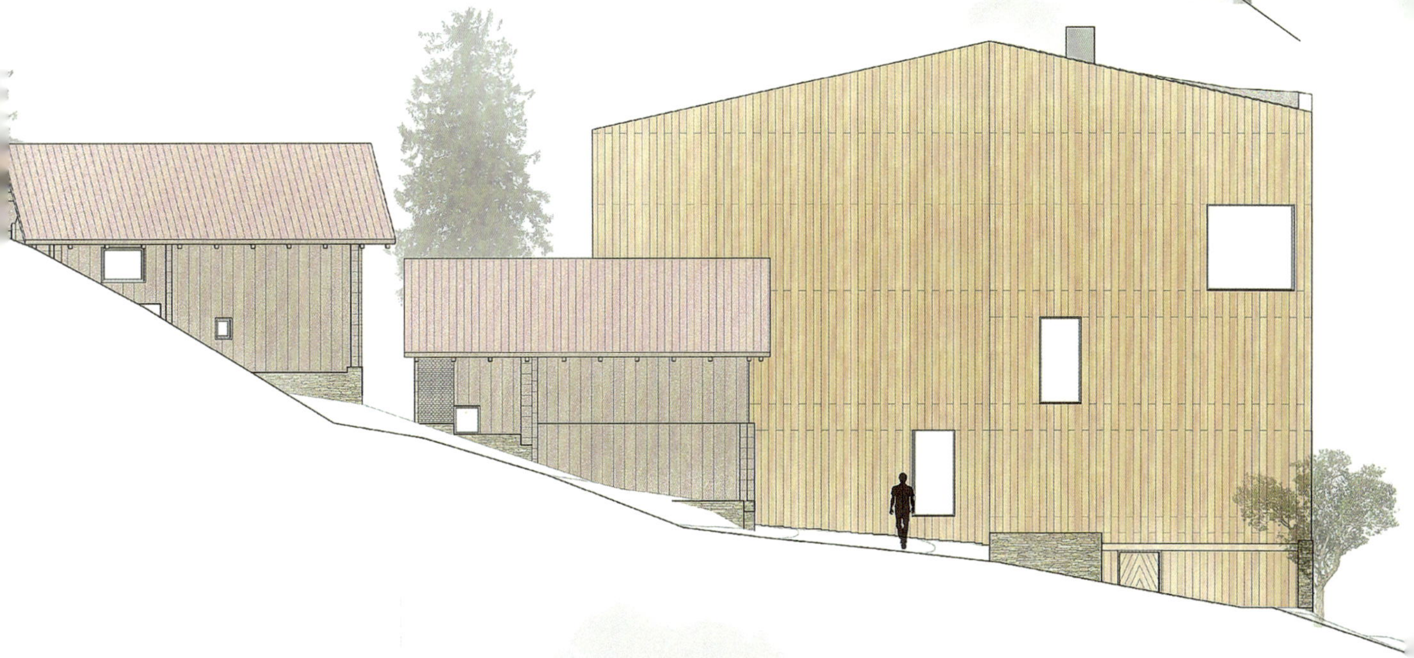

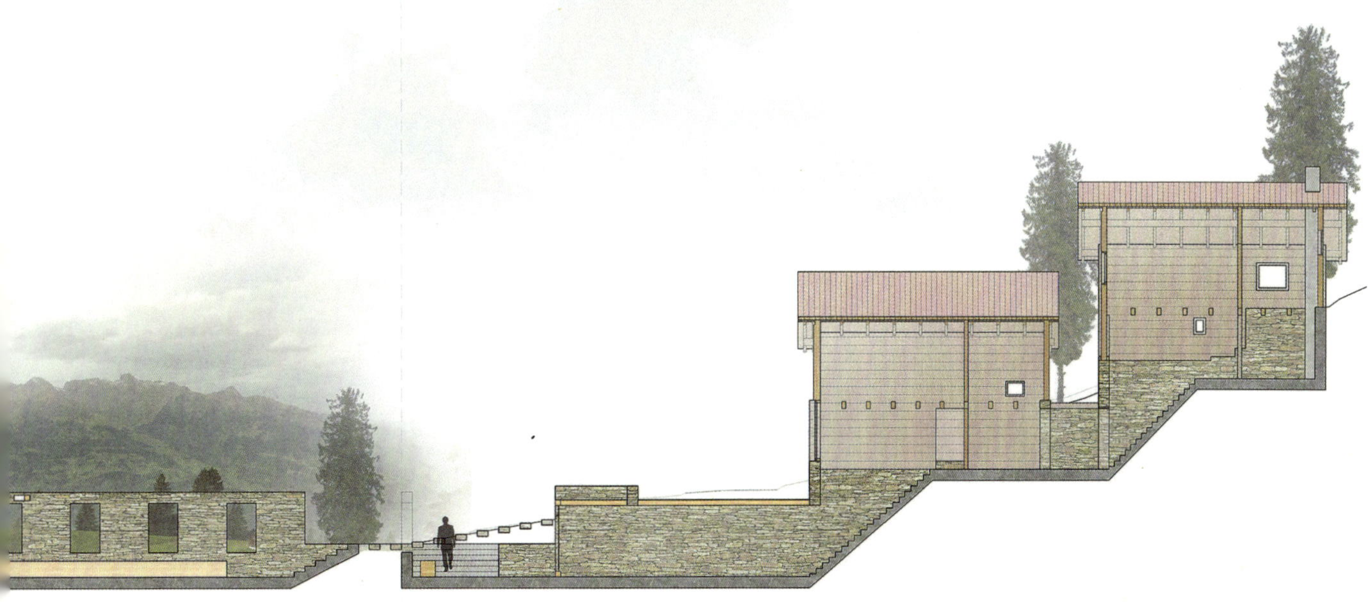

Sanctuary

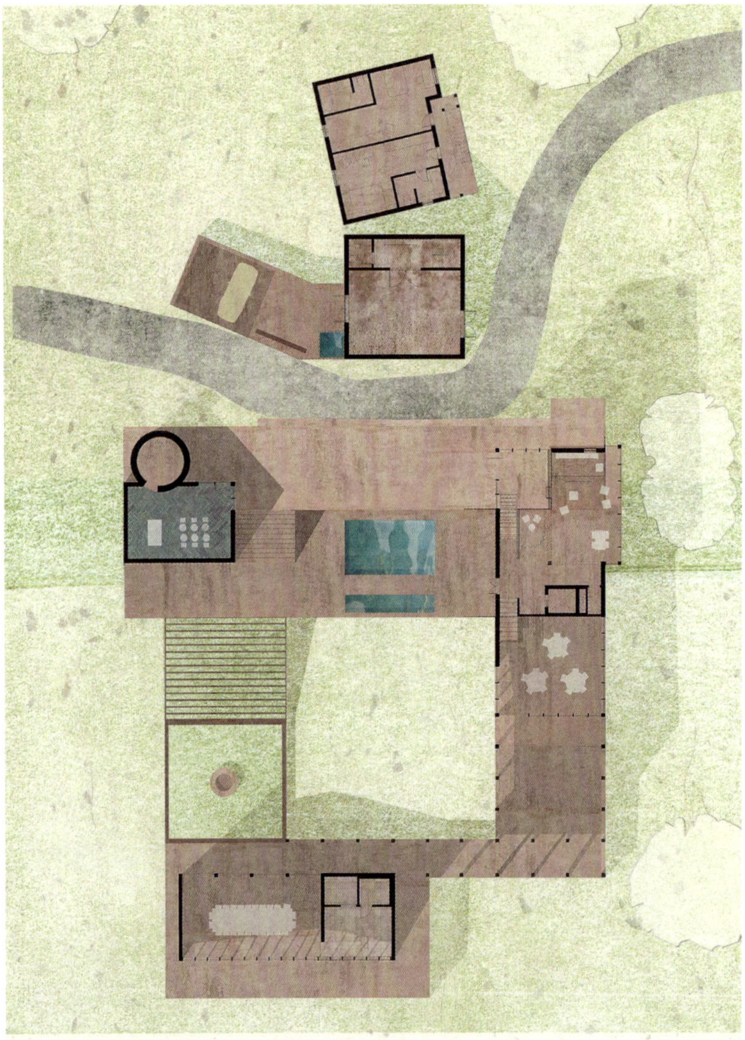

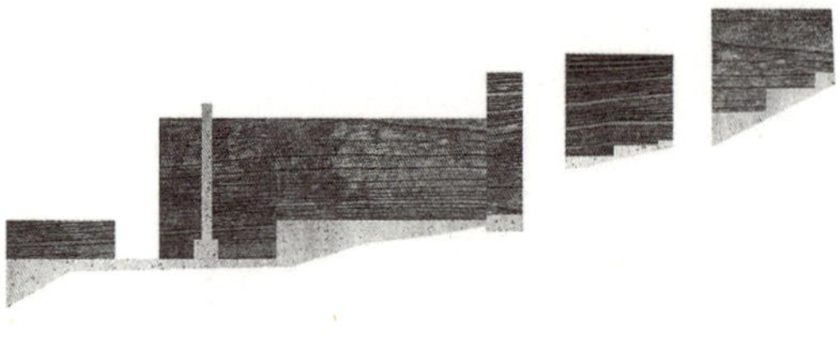

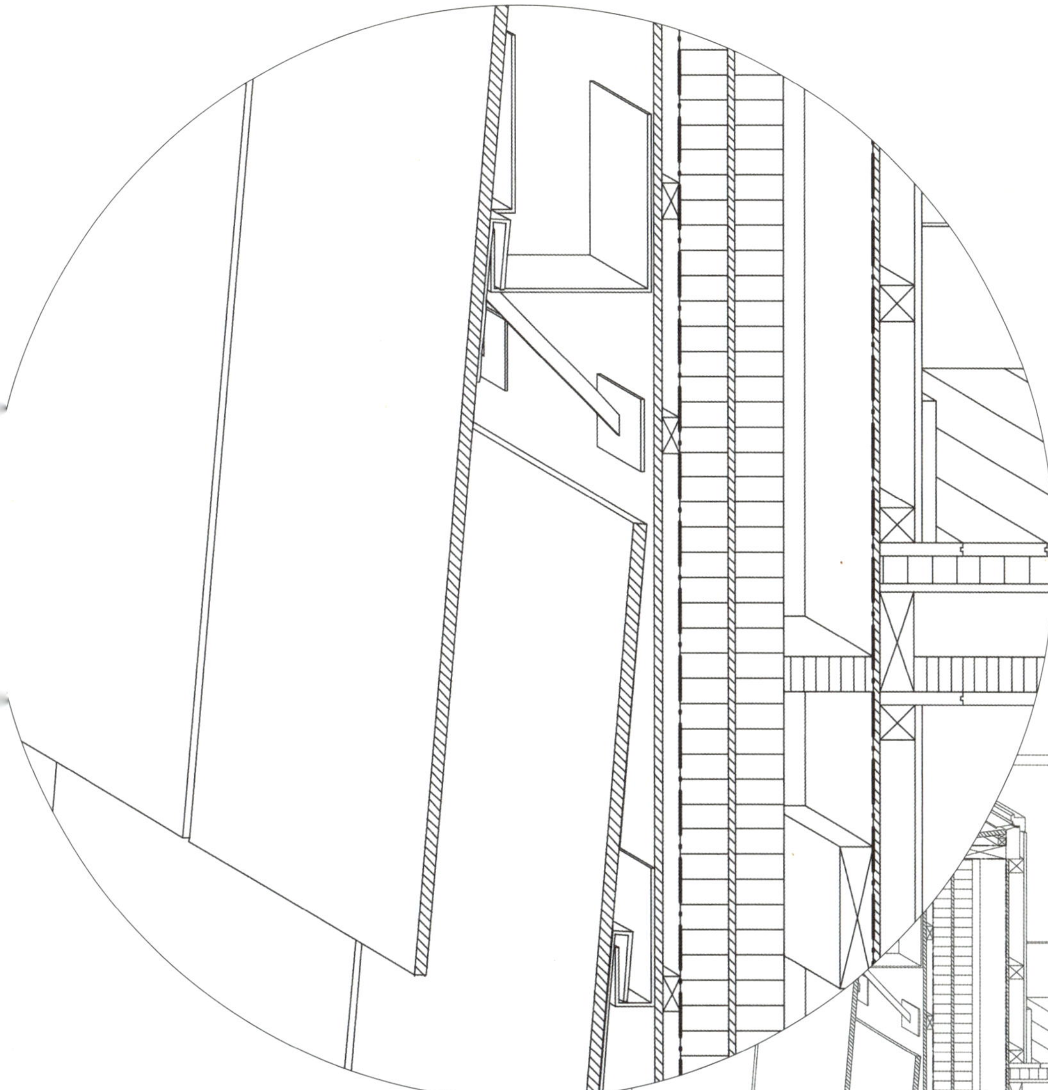

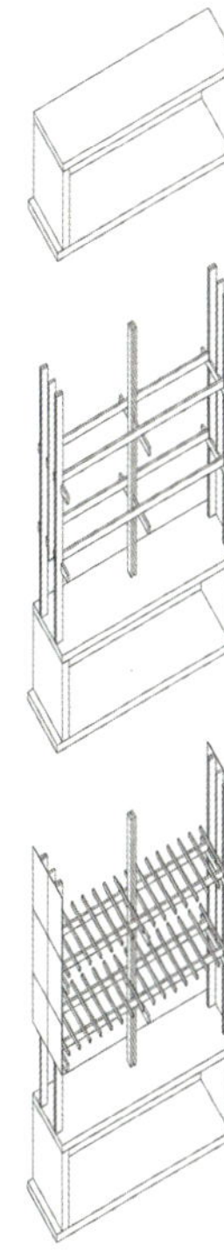

1:20

Sanctuary

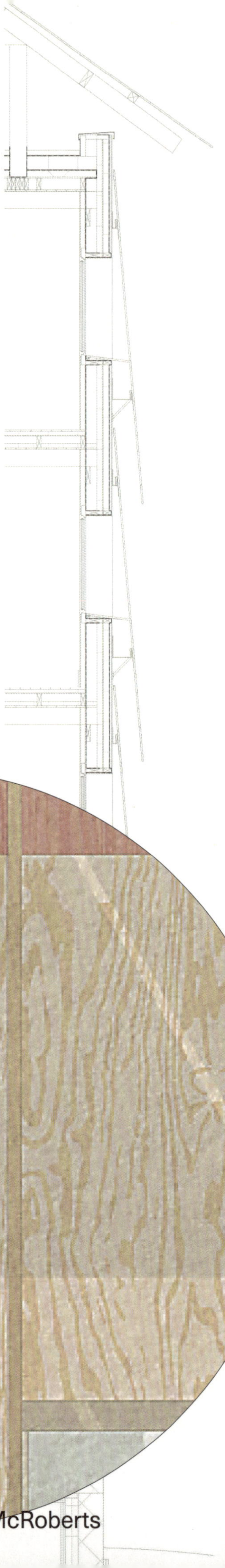

4 CRAFTING STONE, BRICK AND WOOD HANDS-ON

Bricks of the Future

achiel Spaan

'Crafting the Façade' teaches students to draw on tradition in setting innovation in motion. The subtitle 'Reuse, Reinvent, Reactivate' anticipates both current and future situations. Reuse analyses existing constructions, components and building material. Reactivate explores traditions in craftsmanship and technical aspects. Reinvent tackles existing buildings to understand the potential they present.

Clay, stone and wood are natural building materials that we harvest from the earth. In the past, we used these materials locally: brick in the European deltas, stone near the geologically shaped mountains, and wood in and around the forests. People developed local techniques and crafts that listened to the materials. All three—wood, stone and brick—are originally self-supporting structures, each with its own distinctive techniques of stacking and connecting. Since the industrial revolution, building technology has evolved towards hybrid structures in which façades are no longer fully self-supporting. An important reason for this is the need to insulate buildings. Façade structures of brick, stone and wood evolved from solid walls into cleverly composed barriers. Local building techniques and crafts have been superseded by nationally operating production and installation companies that innovate with façade systems and shape them to suit their engineering. The stone, wood and brick façades become part of a façade system. The material is attached to a supporting structure of concrete, steel and/or wood.

The Netherlands has a brick tradition. Clay has been collected from the delta for centuries. By the middle of the 19th century, some 800 small brickworks were scattered around the country, all supplying their local area with bricks. Each region had its own colour and type of brick, depending on the local clay and the production methods employed at the factory. Over the course of the 20th century, many of these factories closed. Scaling-up has meant that only twenty brickworks remained in operation by the year 2000. Bricks have become more uniform, less colourful, and standard in shape. And the application of brick is no longer self-evident.

The use of brick received a fresh impetus in the 1990s, spurred on by the designs of Kollhoff in Amsterdam and Siza in The Hague. These two architects demonstrated a new way of using brick, weaving together tradition and modernity. This opened the eyes of many Dutch architects to the quality of a distinctive material. For the past decade, architects and brickyards have been collaborating again on developing innovative applications of crafted bricks. Sustainability plays an increasingly important role in this process. Creating hard and stackable bricks in an oven costs a lot of energy. It is desirable to develop bricks that can be produced with less energy.

As part of the 'Crafting the Façade' project, students from Amsterdam Academy of Architecture worked with three brickyards to develop new uses for brick. We devised and developed bricks that could be produced with less energy or material and that could be stacked or attached in different ways. We drew inspiration from assembly techniques in wood and stone construction. We shared and compared ideas and construction methods. Each brickyard has its own specialities shaped by history, scale and way of working. Den Daas in Winterswijk, located close to the forelands of the River Ijssel, is a big factory, with modern ovens and its own clay depots. The factory mostly manufactures extruded bricks and waterstruck bricks. Zilverschoon in Randwijk, beside the River Rhine, is a small factory with an old oven. Production is not mechanized but manual, and bricks are produced exclusively to order. St. Joris in Besel, close to the River Meuse, is a mid-sized factory with mechanized production, although parts of the process can be done manually. As a result, there is plenty of freedom in defining the shape and finish of bricks.

Students worked at the Den Daas brickyard with designer Baukje Trenning to explore ways to produce lighter bricks. Den Daas has developed its own lightweight bricks that can be clipped together. Hence the name: Clickbrick. In 2007, Den Daas hosted our first Erasmus Workshop that centred on brick. For the 'Crafting the Façade' project, students developed thin bricks. For this, the form and composition of the clay is vital, because the brick should not break while hardening or in the oven. The students then developed methods to stack bricks or attach them together, because traditional bonding courses proved inadequate. Together with an international group of students from Amsterdam, Liechtenstein and Glasgow, we produced numerous bricks. We made moulds, experienced the stiffness of the clay, and felt the heat of the ovens. We developed flattened bricks that reminded us of roof tiles or slates. And long bricks with a hook or curve that made it possible to hang them up.

The bricks are applicable in hybrid façades where construction, insulation and waterproofing are separated from one another. In wood, stone and brick architecture, hybrid façades express an interesting tension between 'supporter and supported'. The brickwork façade is expected to carry the forces to the ground, but in practice this façade hangs like a curtain from a supporting structure. The designer must take this into account.

At the factory in Zilverschoon the focus is not on 'high speed and quantity' but on 'beauty and purity'. This traditional brickyard works on a small scale on restoration projects and on bricks that are not standard in size or surface texture. Hands and moulds are the primary tools. Architect Jochem Heijmans worked with his students on large bricks with natural or mechanical imperfections. The bricks were inspired by the large Roman bricks used in castles and monasteries. Since current regulations make these large bricks unfeasible because of their weight, the students developed lighter bricks such as a 'sponge' brick. The clay is mixed with polystyrene balls that are burned away during the firing process. Adding the right number of balls led to a lighter brick that proved strong enough and could be stacked, and also had a fine natural surface. A second brick was trimmed diagonally to create a pattern of shadows when stacked. A third brick combined two types of clay. The process of adding, cutting and mixing resulted in beautiful textures in the fired clay, which bore similarities to the textures of stone and wood.

The surface of brick bears traces of deposits and fossils. And a sawn log displays annual growth rings and knots. These traces of nature lend the materials a distinctive and 'natural' character by which we recognize them. Bricks also contain natural traces owing to 'pollutants' in the extracted clay, such as iron, loess and marl. These minerals give bricks their distinctive brown, red or yellow tint. When mixing the clay, we can influence these traces by adding more substances or slicing off the outer layer of the bricks. Natural imperfections in the material enhance the quality of the façade.

Brick is an industrial product for St. Joris. The factory manufactures special bricks for windowsills and string courses and often produces glazed finishes. The factory works with product designers like Tom van Soest. Together with the company Stonecycling, they develop bricks that contain waste materials that give them a unique appearance. Stonecycling compares them with food and gives the bricks names like Aubergine and Truffel. Architect Jurgen van der Horst teamed up with Ward Massa of Stonecycling and a group of students to experiment with Westerwalder clay, to which waste substances were added. Students designed and made bricks that could be stacked in clever ways. One brick in the shape of a parallelogram can be stacked in a number of ways to create an open or closed wall. Another brick took the shape of a jigsaw puzzle piece that can be connected to other pieces in a variety of ways. It can be used to build structures that can be dismantled again later.

In addition to the reuse of waste materials in new brickwork, the possibility of taking buildings apart again is becoming increasingly important because it allows for the reuse of construction components. Dismantling has enjoyed a long tradition in wooden structures, as we see with smart joints like the dovetail, mortise and tenon, and tongue and groove. Dismantling is still in its infancy when it comes to brickwork and stone structures. New brick and stone connections lead to buildings with distinctive characteristics.

All bricks designed and produced by students challenge us to play and experiment. This was precisely the aim of 'Crafting the Façade'. Playing and experimenting are how we search for new possibilities using clay, the making and firing process and the method of stacking. In this quest, material, production and application are inextricably linked to one another. Essential questions are reviewed. How to we deal with the tension between 'supporter and supported'? How do we exploit the natural imperfection of a material? How can we create innovative connections and forms of assembly?

We discovered comparable themes as we innovated with brick, wood and stone structures. Making both the production process and the product itself more sustainable was an important motivation: processing the material, making façades lighter, making building components demountable, making smart products that can be manufactured industrially. Traditional values and crafts are a valuable foundation. Knowledge of traditions is important, but so too is looking beyond boundaries. Seeing similarities as well as differences makes us aware of the potential and limitations of materials and techniques. Fully understanding a brick, timber or stone structure teaches each student to take a fresh look at what at first glance might seem a self-explanatory façade.

The Language of the Façade, the Culture of Materials

Sally Stewart

During the symposium that concluded the 'Crafting the Façade' project, I told a story involving material culture, building traditions and the complexity of gaining an expert knowledge at second hand and as an outsider.

As a child, I took part in the annual festival in my home town, which one year required me to be dressed in traditional alpine clothes, one of a number of children on a tableau depicting a famous fictional alpine inn. My dress was made by my mother, a skilled dressmaker, to a traditional pattern supplied by her Austrian friend and using authentic cloth and silver buttons imported for the purpose. As the symposium audience witnessed, while my costume displayed an understand of the original, the authentic, no doubt because of the research and careful attention to detail underpinning it, the structure of the tableau that I stood beside was only a poor substitute for a chalet, with only the slightest similarity in appearance to the real thing, and the critical aspects and qualities of the vernacular typology were lost in translation. While the set of clothes had been made with an understanding of the materials, techniques and culture associated with it, none of the same thinking or understanding had informed the building process. I commented on the fact that it was this searching for understanding underpinning our actions that 'Crafting the Façade' was attempting to achieve.

Working with three materials (Stone, Brick and Wood), three building traditions (Scottish, Dutch and Alpine) and three cities (Glasgow, Amsterdam and Vaduz), the participants in 'Crafting the Façade' have had to confront both our shared bodies of knowledge and our divergent histories, vernacular traditions, cultural and environmental conditions, all of which contribute to the way we choose to design and to build. From Semper to Frampton, while we may have creative practice or traditions that appear to be alike, it requires a careful unravelling of the thinking behind these to see if they are indeed the same or only similar in appearance. Simultaneously, we can discover how divergent our building practices are, growing out of unique traditions and subject to very different contemporary pressures and drivers.

The contemporary dilemma

How then is the student architect to navigate this complex and critical territory, able to understand a far wider range of available contemporary tectonic possibilities than in previous times, while recognizing the contribution and continuity that architecture and the built form make to wider society? How can the student architect learn to act as an insider rather than remain an outsider when their education and future practice is unlikely to be rooted in one place? These may be modern dilemmas brought about by the possibilities to study and practice at a distance from your origins, and the distancing of the architect from the building process as a result of contemporary procurement, but without recognizing these challenging circumstances, we risk, as architects, being on the periphery of the discussion, while we should be equipped to contribute to it at its centre.

Within the Mackintosh School, there is a recognition that within the academy we have to compensate for the distance between the architecture students and the practice they are trying to develop. We recognize that building tectonic and construction insights can be achieved in many different ways, through sources that provide not just facts or solutions but through a connected narrative that helps assimilate the full scope of the knowledge such as in the case of *Constructing Architecture*[1], a rare textbook that bridges technology, culture and practice. We also recognize that if the studio is seen as the heart of the education, then design projects must provide opportunities to discuss tectonics as creative drivers within design, a welcome guest at the table rather than an additional constraint. For this approach to become embedded, we must make it part of our regular way of thinking and acting, "the recognized processes of iteration and reflection that underpin studio education cannot be fast tracked, and few models have emerged that ultimately equip the architect on their journey to belonging a master of their craft".[2] We also recognize that even aligning the curriculum to meet our ambitions and achieving an integrated practice is complex and challenging, especially when in a university based education, the opportunities to encounter the act of building become few and far between.[3]

Crafting a project

'Crafting the Façade' provided a structure for both teachers and students to confront the wicked problem of how we should build now, and how we can equip ourselves to do this even at the beginning of an architectural education. The project structure and its contributing elements also provided a means to be able to triangulate (or oscillate) between the three key strands of programme—context and technology or typology, topology and tectonics—and to understand better the dynamic potential existing between these.

The focus on the façade acted as a device to concentrate thinking on the most prominent and therefore loaded aspect of any building, literally and conceptually, where the poche or envelope simultaneously consists of the internal and external surfaces we encounter, mediates climate and provides identity.[4]

Stone

Heavy massive materials can be difficult to play with. In order to be able to explore the nature of stone, the prevailing building material that has shaped Scotland's urban centres, in designing the Glasgow workshop, a certain amount of lateral thinking was required. The material does not lend itself to be modelled in a miniaturized form, and unlike other modular materials there is only so much that can be learnt in a short period of time from stacking or similar techniques that do not require the advanced skills of the mason. To complicate the situation further, contemporary masonry façades are seldom load-bearing or use traditional building techniques, requiring detective work to understand how the façade has been realized.

Investigating twelve stone façades within the city, students were encouraged to draw and speculate on the construction of the façades they were allotted, using the observation, surveying, building history and information on architectural period as clues. Drawings grew in size to better represent the scale of the original façades, and to understand the combination of stone courses and usually mortar joints, until the scale most appropriate was established at 1:10. These enormous drawings, drawn by hand, also challenged the students' normal approach to drawing. Collaborative and speculative by nature, the laptop was no longer locus of the drawing. Instead, long tables or walls were needed to give sufficient area to work on, several people drafting at once. The technique stuck, and in subsequent workshops and design

1 Andrea Deplazes, *Constructing Architecture: Materials, Processes, Structures: A Handbook*, Birkhäuser, 2005.

2 Sally Stewart, 'Insider not Outsider; Integrating Environmental Thinking in Thesis Design', 2011, In: *Teaching a new environmental culture: the environment as a question of architectural education*, EAAE Transactions on Architectural Education (53). EAAE ENHSA, Thessaloniki, pp. 391–397. ISBN 978-2-930301-51-8.

3 Both the Amsterdam Academy and Mackintosh School have routes to degrees that allow students to work in practice while studying, giving the potential for experiencing building realized over a sustained period. The University of Liechtenstein provides intensive immersive opportunities for students to build from the first years of its degree, acknowledging the importance of this experience.

4 The thread continued directly in MSA from the lectures of Professor Isi Metzstein, who took great pleasure in comparing the Great Pyramid at Giza with the Domino House as extreme examples of poche or the absence of it.

reviews, students were asked to draw their façade proposals at 1:10, giving them a significant and striking physical presence.

The project also proposed the bookending of the intensive study of a material, beginning with a shared workshop week involving a small group of students from each of the three participating schools, and finishing with a symposium that offered the opportunity of discussion and dissemination to a wider group of students, and in the case of Stone, to staff and student visitors too. In contrast to the workshop which provided an extended immersion into the culture, physics and technology of stone, the symposium provided a taste of the variety of ways stone could be explored, discussed and deployed and later pursued by the individual.

One positive aspect of the symposium that was not foreseen was the potential for students to present to each other research work they had undertaken into the subject, and possibilities for peer-to-peer learning beyond the original workshop participants. An example of this, 'Ode for the stone'[5], presented by a collaborative student team from Luca, Ghent, provided a vivid account of the diverse range of techniques and tactics used to develop strategies supporting the conservation of a historic abbey, including surveys, drawings, castings, collages, collections and engravings, all of which focused on the material qualities of the stone, and formed the counterpoint to the description of the behaviour of stone within the first Mackintosh building fire presented by an experienced construction professional.

Conclusions

Our final symposium in Vaduz in May 2017 provided a chance to scan across our three materials, academies and approaches. Perhaps the most unexpected outcome of the project was the ability to consider three common materials, their tectonic qualities and associated building practice and culture, and to provoke a vivid and energised discussion of architecture. This undoubtedly was based on the connections, relationships and understanding that develops when working at close quarters with each other and over a sustained period of time. We, too, have contributed in some small way to the discussion of the language of the façade, the culture of materials. We, too, eventually became insiders and no longer outsiders.

5 Lampaert, Matteo, Dhont, Miel, Qunitellier, Aurike, *Ode for the Stone—Anastyloses*, Guest lecture, Stone Symposium, 23 September 2016, The Glasgow School of Art.

Collaborative Teaching

atherine Li, Robert Mantho

Workshops where students and staff from multiple schools of architecture collaborate offer a wide range of intellectually engaging and educationally valuable benefits, both academic and architectural, for students and staff, especially if participants come from different cultures. The value to students of direct learning through hands-on work at scale 1:1 is wide-ranging, with the added benefit of providing opportunities and challenges for the development of teaching practices.

Collaborative projects raise numerous issues that require participants to call on skills related to the specialist knowledge of architectural design methodology, as well as interpersonal exchange. To collaborate effectively, a context of trust and openness is essential, and building the structures which facilitate this is the key task for staff designing collaborative activities. Working with a group from across Europe involves cultural exchange that encourages an environment of curiosity and exposure to alternative approaches for all participants.

This type of knowledge exchange is beneficial not only because of the acquisition of information and techniques, but also because it highlights the value of intellectual pliability. Comprehending how various solutions address specific challenges, and evaluating the strengths and weaknesses, extends knowledge and clarifies the core principles involved in specific design problems. While there is no doubt that collaborative projects face significant challenges, particularly if they involve cross-cultural exchange, it is also clear that these are far outweighed by the numerous professional and educational outcomes derived from such projects. What follows is a brief discussion of the challenges encountered and the benefits this mode of operation can provide to all participants.

Cultural exchange

'Crafting the Façade' limited the exploration of materiality at 1:1 to stone, brick and wood. These choices were based on the dominant architectural material in each country. This provides an environment of learning which tethers the practicality of the material to cultural heritage, which helps to embed architectural experience in the learning of participants.

'Crafting the Façade' was comprised of three European institutions in the UK, the Netherlands and Liechtenstein. Each university provided staff and students from the home country, but the teams also included students from further afield. The participating nationalities ranged from Thailand, Norway and America to Australia, India and China, while only four of the Glasgow contingent were native Scots. This contributed to a diverse and rich cultural input into the academic and social components of the project.

Benefits of 1:1 work

Jonathan Swift wrote that 'Elephants are always drawn smaller than life, but a flea always larger'.[1] Architects very much design between

1 Jonathan Swift (1703), 'Thoughts on Various Subjects', in *The Prose Writings of Jonathan Swift*, ed. Herbert Davis and others, 16 vols. (Oxford: Basil Blackwell, 1939–74), vol. i, pp. 241–5, 303.

these parameters and frequently do not encounter full scale until they reach the construction phase. Swift's elephant has no notional size today. We are not constrained by the size of a piece of paper, having been afforded the ability by current computer software to zoom in and out of 'model space' at will. If we are lucky, a client may fund the production of sample panels to test and verify ideas before moving to final construction details, but this is the exception rather than the norm. An architect therefore might only gain a knowledge of the tectonics of materials through a built body of work, well after leaving university.

If students can produce photorealistic images conjured up in an afternoon on the computer, how do they gain a true understanding of materiality, construction and scale while in academia? On most architectural courses this is explored through a mix of model-making, visits to completed buildings, and lectures in technology. Students will supplement this with inspiration gained via online media and images accessed through Google. The focus on exploration through model-making is a mainstay of teaching and learning across all three of the 'Crafting the Façade' institutions.

In this digital age the demand by students to gain experience from hands-on 'live build', working at 1:1, is ever increasing. This is demonstrated by the proliferation of projects such as Mackay Lyons Sweet Apple 'Ghost',[2] Tom Emerson's 'Pavilion of Reflections'[3] and Hello Wood's educational workshops.[4] Is this perhaps a reaction to the constraints of the computer? Students gain valuable experience by feeling the weight and texture of materials in their hands and the workability of each of them. The three-dimensional quality of construction connections and junctions, down to the precise choice of bolt in order create an elegant detail, is not easily taught in the studio environment, but is quickly understood by students on site. This is Pallasmaa's thinking hand in action.[5]

Unlike some 'live build' projects where the design is fully in the hands of the organizers or the outcomes are in a single material, 'Crafting the Façade' investigated the properties of three materials over four iterations and had no predefined design outcomes. This added to the richness of the project by allowing participants to learn not only from their own particular investigations but also from those produced by other groups within the cohort. This was the strength of the project. As William McRoberts, one of the students from Glasgow commented, 'It's the physicality of holding something in your hand; you get to really know the joint'.[6] The mix of part-time masters students from Amsterdam and full-time undergraduate students from Glasgow and Vaduz enabled the more professionally experienced students to share knowledge with their younger counterparts. Students from Glasgow cite the exposure to the studio cultures of the different institutions as an important factor in their own understanding of their individual learning and gave them a better perspective on GSA's pedagogic structure.

The advantage for staff on any 1:1 build is the ability to fully engage with students on the task, which is not easily achieved during normal studio discourse. Physically sharing the design experience can level the pedagogic relationship, whereby students feel more autonomy in developing their line of enquiry. In 'Crafting the Façade,' staff were able to gain vital knowledge of regional and national differences in construction techniques, enhanced by field trips and examinations of the 1:10 drawing studies. Alpine methods of *blockbau* and *strickbau* in timber construction are not normally taught in the Netherlands or Scotland, so students from those countries gained a wider perspective of what we might call European 'archi-culture'. This is something which will benefit not only the staff's studio teaching but also their studio practices.

The differences between the pedagogic approaches of each institution also become evident through this type of cultural exchange, and the logistics of organizing the project across three institutions can be challenging. Glasgow School of Art has a flat year structure. All students move through a sequential academic path, following the same syllabus, and cohorts can be up to 100 students in size. Liechtenstein also works in years, but students are able to choose 'units' after their first year, with about 15 taking part in each. Amsterdam is run as a part-time masters course, with similar-sized cohorts to those in Liechtenstein. Knitting the diversity together was always going to be difficult. The true benefits of the 1:1 is the joy of collective making, the production of something real that has impact outside the confines of the studio.

Benefits of collaboration

Collaboration as a design methodology has a range of benefits, particularly in relation to architectural education.[7] By providing a context of interaction, where all contributions are considered with equal weight and participants share their individual perspectives to build a collective response, collaborative processes generate robust design outcomes. 'Crafting the Façade' was established to capitalize on the expertise of the participating institutions, to enrich their individual educational cultures, and to contribute to the collective body of knowledge across the network of European schools of architecture.

Through a series of exercises, with a set of making prompts, the three groups each worked with a single material: wood, brick and stone. The workshop utilized interaction as a key device for generating design conversations. Students were guided to directly explore the properties, possibilities and techniques associated with each material. This led to an understanding of the limits and demands of the material through empirical experience. Within the material groups, participants from the different institutions were mixed, so that students with different levels of experience, cultural backgrounds and architectural viewpoints were working together. This facilitated a natural process of exchange with guidance from tutors. These exchanges helped the groups to construct a set of principles and avenues for exploration.

Continued interaction exercises furthered the goal of creating a set of shared design objectives, by having the group cycle through a series of options and to critically evaluate them using the pool of concepts developed collectively. Interaction was extended through a series of presentations across the groups, with each material group explaining the work, the outcomes of their investigations and their ultimate design responses. This practice of interaction ensured that once construction began the whole group supported the proposed designs and that these had been critiqued from multiple viewpoints. Consequently, the resulting solutions were well considered and possessed sound design logic related to one another. Moreover, they provided a coherent architectural experience that was strongly connected to the site.

A key aspect of collaborative projects is the development of trust.[8] Without trust, it is difficult to arrive at solutions and maintain the motivation required to construct meaningful full-size architectural proposals, particularly if the time frame is condensed. The three days spent exploring the material and finding a design solution to be constructed helped the group to generate the trust required to accomplish the final outcome. The short duration of each workshop and the ambition to construct full-scale designs meant that everyone spent a great deal of time together, with communal meals and demanding physical experiences. This resulted in an intensity which created a unique atmosphere, both challenging and pleasurable. Working in this way requires focus and trust, compelling the group to overcome difficulties and learn to rely on one another to achieve their goals. With this trust comes a willingness to accept contributions with significant differences, allowing students to see a colleague's view of a problem or aesthetic interest as valuable. This gives students the important insight that expanding their field of approaches is beneficial and helps them to develop their ability to investigate architecture.

Conclusion

The collaborative teaching methodologies and 'live build' experience used in the 'Crafting the Façade' project generated considerable benefits for both students and teaching teams. Students gained invaluable knowledge about material properties and direct understanding of complex three-dimensional conditions, both of which are difficult to apprehend through drawing and scale models. Staff could demonstrate and model design strategies and techniques with a clarity and tangibility

2 Juhani Pallasmaa, *The Thinking Hand: Existential and Embodied Wisdom in Architecture*, John Wiley & Sons 2009.

3 Mackay Lyons' Sweet Apple 'Ghost'. https://www.archdaily.com/119109/ghost-7-mackay-lyons-sweetapple-architects [Accessed 20.11.17]

4 Tom Emerson, ETH Zurich for Manifesta 11, the nomadic European biennial. https://www.archdaily.com/790430/pavilion-of-reflections-studio-tom-emerson [Accessed 20.11.17]

5 Hello Wood's educational workshops, http://www.hellowood.eu/ [Accessed 20.11.17]

6 'Crafting the Façade Interviews', short film produced by Glasgow participants.

7 David Dunster, 'Collaboration in Education: The Diploma Project at the Bartlett School, 1988–89', *Journal of Architectural Education (1984–)* 43, no. 2 (1990): pp. 14–21.

8 R. Mantho, 'Constructing Trust in Collaboration', *Architecture and Culture*, V6N1 Taylor & Francis, Abingdon, U.K. Ed. Jessica Kelly.

much more readily, with the concrete engagement strengthening the communication of challenging abstract knowledge. Working with a group of people to achieve a common goal allowed participants to develop insights and skills as individuals and as part of a group. Collaboration demonstrates the benefits of interaction, revealing the extension of understanding that results from exchange between individuals. The 'Crafting the Façade' workshops emphasized the role that trust plays in the design process, as well as in producing high-quality outcomes. Students learned to listen and communicate respectfully, and tutors expanded their range of teaching approaches and architectural knowledge.

Interpersonal skills and communication were central to the success of this collaborative project, giving students important experience in working with other designers and exposure to diverse approaches to design problems. Staff strengthened knowledge networks and built relationships that can develop new research and collaborative opportunities. The cultural exchange of the 'Crafting the Façade' collaboration is a key objective of the Erasmus programme, revealing the common principles that operate across the specifics of language and individual material cultures. Everyone involved learns new techniques and increases the breadth of their design repertoires, testing new design ideas and sharing and experiencing varied teaching strategies that support the collaborative exercise. The depth and range of academic knowledge and experience generated by the 'Crafting the Façade' project is testament to the value of bringing together staff and students from three European schools of architecture and demonstrates the usefulness of collaborative teaching methodologies, and the power of working together to learn and make.

Workshops

Stone

10–17.10.2015
Glasgow

Brick

16–20.03.2016
Azewijn

Wood

11–16.10.2016
Vaduz

Closing Workshop

25–31.08.2017
Voerendaal

Four workshops for all participants from the three schools ran in the three countries. The goal of each workshop, which was an essential part of the project studio, was to become familiar with one material and its properties, and with the building culture of the region. During the stone, brick and wood workshops, participants first surveyed historical buildings constructed of one of the three materials, and then worked in teams to draw sections and elevations by hand at scale 1:10. In the second part of the workshops, students studied structural elements at scale 1:1. During the final workshop they experimented and built with stone, brick and wood at the same time.

The workshops consisted of two parts which both gave access to first-hand material experiences. After the analytical part, in which large-scale research drawings were created by hand in multinational groups, the material was used in hands-on sessions in full-scale prototypes.

Stone

During the stone workshop we decided to make 1:10 detail drawing through the façades of selected ten-storey stone buildings in th centre of Glasgow. Realizing that big drawings were essential in help ing students gain insight into the qualities of stone, we came to under stand that working at a large scale echoed the difficulties of workin with stone. Such difficulties could only be overcome by dedicatio and commitment to the task at hand, and by acquiring knowledge developing skills and applying techniques—in essence, masterin a form of craftsmanship akin to that of the stonemason. Shifting th scale of drawing clarified the core value of the workshop, offerin students fundamental insight into the craft of making a stone build ing and making a hand drawing. Just as importantly, it underline the role of drawings as instruments of knowledge that fuse the con ception and construction of buildings. The shift in scale also marke a dramatic increase in production, heralding the creation of drawing of a size alien to a generation of students restricted by the limits o their computer screens. Such large drawings required students t develop new skills and techniques, to master new materials suc as charcoal and new drafting tools to construct large drawing sur faces, and to use timber battens to compose the final drawing. I the process, students discovered the value of the drawing as a crafte object unmediated by the computer.

Brick

As part of the 'Crafting the Façade' project, students from the Am sterdam Academy of Architecture worked with three brickyards t develop new uses for brick. Together they devised and develope bricks that could be produced with less energy or material and tha could be stacked or attached in different ways. Each brickyard ha its own specialities shaped by history, scale and way of working Den Daas in Winterswijk, located close to the forelands of the Rive IJssel, is a big factory with modern ovens and its own clay deposits The factory mostly manufactures extruded bricks and waterstruc bricks. Zilverschoon in Randwijk, beside the River Rhine, is a sma factory with an old oven. Production is not mechanized but manua and bricks are produced exclusively to order. St. Joris in Besel, clos to the River Meuse, is a mid-sized factory with mechanized produc tion, although parts of the process can be done manually. As a resul there is plenty of freedom in defining the shape and finish of bricks The results were exhibited at the outdoor Exposition FabCity 201 in Amsterdam and at Dutch Design Week 2016 in Eindhoven.

16–20.03.2016
Azewijn

Wood

In the wood workshop students used timber planks and small beam
to construct components that could serve as both roofs and wall
Eight groups worked on various lamella structures with which t
construct a pointed arch roof to cover an area of 5 by 16 metres. A
a reference, they used the so-called 'Zollingerdach', an efficient an
expressive rhomboid structure made up of generic component
Participants first built eight different prototypes at scale 1:10 befor
constructing them at full scale to define the shape of a future buil
ing. The constructions were remarkably different in their tectoni
and structural conception and presented an inspiring range of sol
tions. They underlined the experimental nature of the whole proje
and marked the starting point for the design and building proces
of the new model workshop at the University of Liechtenstein, whic
students built on campus in the summer of 2017.

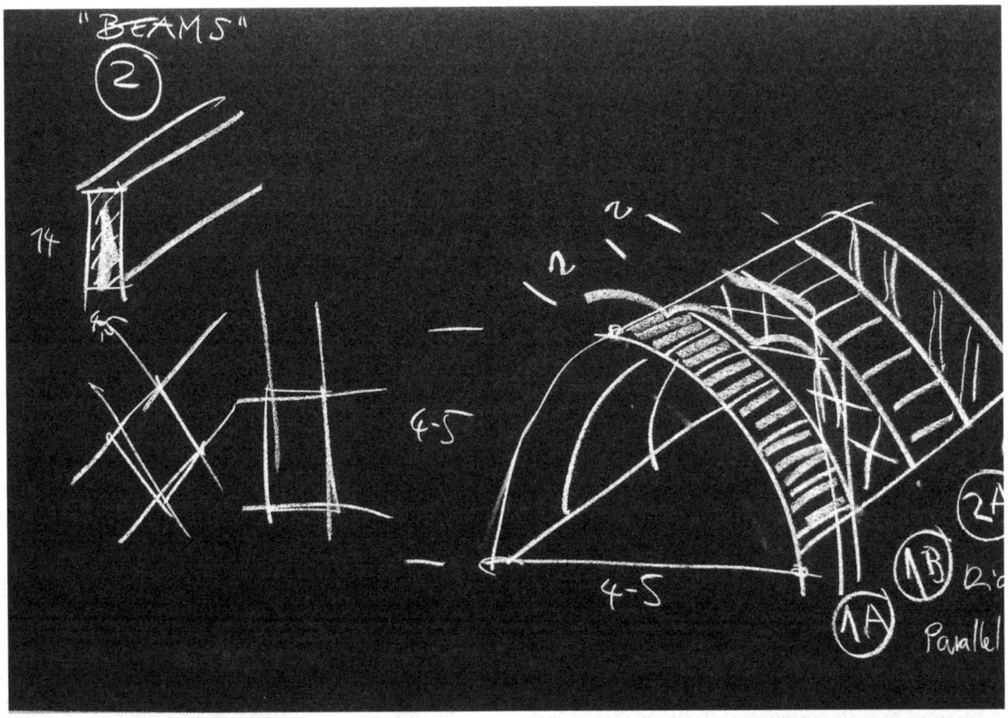
"BEAMS"
2
14
4-5
4-5
1A
1B
2A
Parallel

Kunz
5t

Closing Workshop

Working with three location-specific materials, participants invest
gated the relationship between façade and building. For the fin
workshop in August 2017, the parallel studios travelled to the Fron
berg vineyard in Limburg, in the south of the Netherlands, and bui
with the three materials. This region is home to various castles, cloi
ters and farmhouses built in a combination of stone, brick and timbe
Stone is extracted from a local Kunradersteen quarry, bricks are fire
from clay from the River Maas, and timber is harvested from loc
forests. The workshop took place on a geological site where studen
could experiment freely with the available materials in ways th
opened their eyes, surprised them and tempted them to take ne
steps in the design process. The experiments with the three materia
resulted in three small spatial objects in stone, brick and timber.

25–31.08.2017
Voerendaal

Participants

Workshops and Studios

Stone, 2015–16

Students:
Eric Goldhoorn
Joeri van Wijk
Mick Madder
Olivier Hortentius
Casper van Deelen
Erik Brusse
Haidar Al-Dayri
Ries van den Bosch
Segio Dias
Ivo Clason
Pandelis Zarakovitis
Philip Daniel Shores
Manuela Türtscher
Milena Fischer
Elena Längle
Sabine Makovec
Bettina Ruepp
Barbara Ruech
Janine Alge
Stephanie Rattanong
Leslie Ospelt
Itana Celtic
Michael Hohenadl
Bastian Nenning
Gian-Andrea Beer
Werner Ostermann
Siti Hannah Basalamah
Ren P'ng
Ewan Wotherspoon
Stefanie Schnetzer
Yu Xuan Qua
Joe Duffin
Gabriela Wäger
Lewis Kane
Toby Lindo
Andy Jack
Jerome Wren
Weng Yi Wong

Teachers:
Carmen Rist-Stadelmann
Urs Meister
Machiel Spaan
Dingeman Deijs
Wouter Kroeze
Sally Stewart
Alan Hooper
Neil Mochrie
Neil Simpson

Brick, 2016

Students:
Andre Cramer
Arne de Gans
Juliette Gilson
Koen van Hoof
Thom Knubben
Kristina Košić
Stefan Koster
Hoeshmand Mahmoed
Jesse Mommers
Lucas Pissetti
Karolis Platakis
Bram Ruarus
Lu Yu
Carl Baker
Matthew Healy
Ziyang Li
Brigit Luffingham
Sandra Magrath
David Mcpike
Segoline Morand
Agata Olszewska
Kirsty Shankland
Fraser Start
Brigitte Baier
Ewelina Langer
Maximilian Kindle
Viviane Göbel
Christina Wieser
Maximilian Kaufmann
Manuel Moser
Valerie Rainer

Teachers:
Carmen Rist-Stadelmann
Urs Meister
Machiel Spaan
Wouter Kroeze
Jan Peter Wingender
Udo Garitzman
Baukje Trenning
Jochem Heijmans
Jurjen van der Horst
Ward Massa
Alan Hooper
Neil Mochrie
Robert Mantho

Wood, 2016–17

Students:
Philipp Althammer
Christoph Ammer
Julia Beck
Pascale Büchel
Christoph Fessler
Julia Forrer
Livia Herle
Daniela Huber
Julia Mair
Lino Nägele
Anne-Lea Pfistner
Denise Pfleger
Michelle Rheinberger
Simon Westreicher
Stefan Koster
Roxana Vakil Mozafari
Wouter van der Velpen
Paulien van der Valk
Salaheddine Chekh Ibrahim
Eldrich Piqué
Tristen Vreugdenhil
Dirk Overduin
Joeri Verhoeven
Midas van Boekel
Alexander Beeloo
Eva Souren
Kristina Kosic
Laurence de Kort
Martin Zizka
William McRoberts
Angus Riddell
Pavandip Sian
Ewan Hepburn
Mate Gehberger
Annie Higham
Fredrik Frendin
Nichole Samson
Siripat Rojnirun
Ingrid Wennemo
Rebecca Hodolava

Teachers:
Carmen Rist-Stadelmann
Urs Meister
Machiel Spaan
Wouter Kroeze
Dingeman Deijs
Kathy Li
Anna Poston

Stone, Brick, Wood Closing Workshop, 2017

Students:
Yu Yulu
Casper van Deelen
Dafne Wiegers
Eric Goldhoorn
Tristen Vreugdenhil
Alexander Beelo
Rosa Jonkman
Roel van Loon
Jako Hurkmans
Olivier Lodder
Nina Kater
Ruben Dahmen
Joanne Tschenett
Sarah Juliana Schädler
Lara Anina Schmid
Seraina Bernegger
Ruben De Sa
Ellena Chiara Joanna Neff
Andreas Brandstetter
Serena Keller
Chiara Maria Jug
Sara Manuela Thöny
Liam Cooke
Charles Dunn
Subashini Ganandran
Ewan Hepburn
Justina Jakubkaite
Timothy Khoo
Toby Lindo
Vivien Neoh
Nichole-Ann Samson
Ingrid Wennemo

Teachers:
Carmen Rist-Stadelmann
Urs Meister
Machiel Spaan
Wouter Kroeze
Jan-Richard Kikkert
Kathy Li
Robert Mantho

Inge Beckel
Graduated as an architect from the ETH Zurich, where she wrote her PhD. She worked at the Building Department of the City of Zurich and was editor of the Swiss architecture journal TEC21. She is a freelance architecture publisher with an interface to gender studies, and she also works as a consultant and property representative from her base in Winterthur and Fürstenaubruck.

Alan Hooper
Graduated from the University of Glasgow as a Bachelor of Architecture (Honours) and Master of Architecture. He is senior lecturer and programme leader at the Mackintosh School of Architecture at Glasgow School of Art.

Anne Isopp
Studied architecture at Graz University of Technology and journalism at Danube University Krems. She writes about architecture for newspapers and architectural magazines and is editor-in-chief of Vienna-based *Zuschnitt* magazine, which presents current trends in timber building.

Katherine Li
Graduated from Heriot Watt University in Edinburgh, and has worked for a women's housing association in London and for Gareth Hoskins Architects in Glasgow. She has been teaching since 2003 and is currently Stage 2 leader at the Mackintosh School of Architecture, Glasgow School of Art.

Ranald Macinnes
Graduated in History of Art and Politics at the University of Glasgow. He is Head of Place and Publishing at Historic Environment Scotland in Edinburgh, Honorary Senior Research Fellow of the Institute of Art History, University of Glasgow, and a visiting lecturer at the University of Strathclyde, Department of Architecture.

Robert Mantho
Graduated as an architect from the Architectural Association School of Architecture in London. He has practiced professionally in London, New York, Portland and Vermont. He is currently Stage 4 Leader at the Mackintosh School of Architecture, Glasgow School of Art.

Urs Meister
Graduated in architecture from the ETH Zurich. He is a professor of design and construction at the Institute of Architecture and Planning at the University of Liechtenstein, coordinator of the Erasmus+ program 'Crafting the Façade', and partner of the architecture office Käferstein & Meister Architekten AG in Zurich.

Arjen Oosterman
Works as a critic, educator and curator with a background in architectural history. He is editor-in-chief of *Volume Magazine*. He teaches architectural history, research and writing at several Dutch universities. He has also written, edited and contributed to books on contemporary Dutch architecture. In addition to lecturing, moderating and curating exhibitions at home and abroad, he contributed to Dutch television documentaries and has been a member of several award juries.

Carmen Rist-Stadelmann
Graduated in architecture from the Technical University Vienna and completed her doctoral degree at the same university in 2015. She has practiced professionally in Austria and Malaysia. She is a senior lecturer at the Institute of Architecture and Planning at the University of Liechtenstein and coordinator of the Erasmus+ programme 'Crafting the Façade'.

Marko Sauer
Holds a Master's Degree in Architecture from the University of Liechtenstein and a Bachelor of Secondary Education from the College of Education in St. Gallen. He worked with Staufer & Hasler Architekten in Frauenfeld, at the Department of Construction in St. Gallen, and as editor of the architecture journal *TEC21*. He is also editor-in-chief of *Modulør* magazine in Zurich.

Machiel Spaan
Graduated in architecture from Eindhoven University of Technology. From 2007 to 2013 he was head of architecture at the Amsterdam Academy of Architecture, where he still teaches. With his Amsterdam-based architecture firm M3H Architects, he designs and constructs buildings within existing urban structures.

Sally Stewart
Graduated from the University of Glasgow with a Bachelor of Architecture (Honours) and Master of Architecture. She is a Reader in Architectural Education and Practice, and Head of the Mackintosh School of Architecture at the Glasgow School of Art.

Indira Van 'T Klooster
Studied the history of architecture at the University of Amsterdam and works as a journalist. She is founding editor-in-chief and chair of A10 New European Architecture. Since February 2018 she has been director of the Dudok Centre for Architecture in Hilversum. She has been sat on numerous juries for prizes for young architects, and is regularly invited to lecture all over Europe.

Credits

Editors: Carmen Rist-Stadelmann, Machiel Spaan, Urs Meister
Texts: Inge Beckel, Clarissa Frommelt, Alan Hooper, Anne Isopp, Indira van 't Klooster, Katherine Li, Ranald MacInnes, Robert Mantho, Urs Meister, Arjen Oosterman, Carmen Rist-Stadelmann, Marko Sauer, Stefan Sohler, Machiel Spaan, Sally Stewart
Translation: Billy Noland, David Koralek
Final editing: Billy Noland

Design: SJG / Joost Grootens, Dimitri Jeannottat
Lithography: Marjeta Morinc
Printing: Unicum

ISBN 978-3-03860-101-2

Park Books
Niederdorfstrasse 54
8001 Zurich
Switzerland
www.park-books.com

Printed in the Netherlands

Picture credits:
Base Photography, p. 137
Darko Todorovic, p. 142 (top)
Bruno Klomfar, p. 142 (bottom), p. 143 (both pictures)
Allard van der Hoek, pp. 145–154
All other pictures by teachers and students

Special thanks to:
Clarissa Frommelt and Stefan Sohler, Agentur für Internationale Bildungsangelegenheiten, Vaduz
Frommelt Zimmerei Ing. Holzbau AG, Vaduz
Daas baksteen, Zeddam
Zilverschoon, Randwijk
St Joris Keramische Industrie, Beesel
StoneCycling, Amsterdam
FabCity 2016, Amsterdam
Dutch Design Week 2016, Eindhoven
Facade Beek
Daemen's Houtwarenfabriek, Ubachsberg
Kunrader Steen, Voerendaal
Wijngoed Fromberg
Gemeente Voerendaal
Thierry Goossens
IBA Parkstad, Heerlen

This project has been funded with support from the European Commission. This publication reflects the views only of the author, and the Commission cannot be held responsible for any use which may be made of the information contained therein.

AIBA
Agentur für Internationale Bildungsangelegenheiten
Erasmus+
UNIVERSITÄT LIECHTENSTEIN
Academy of Architecture
Amsterdam University of the Arts
MACKINTOSH SCHOOL OF ARCHITECTURE
THE GLASGOW SCHOOL OF ART

Stone, Brick, Wooc

Closing Workshop
25–31.08.2017
Voerendaal

Symposium
5.05.2017
Vaduz